Kept for the Master's Use

Kept for the Master's Use

By

Frances Ridley Havergal

Bottom of the Hill Publishing

Memphis, TN

www.BottomoftheHillPublishing.com

ISBN: 978-1-61203-074-6

CONTENTS

PREFATORY NOTE

My beloved sister Frances finished revising the proofs of this book shortly before her death on Whit Tuesday, June 3, 1879, but its publication was to be deferred till the Autumn.

In appreciation of the deep and general sympathy flowing in to her relatives, they wish that its publication should not be withheld. Knowing her intense desire that Christ should be magnified, whether by her life or in her death, may it be to His glory that in these pages she, being dead,

'Yet speaketh!'

MARIA V. G. HAVERGAL.

Oakhampton, Worchestershire.

KEPT FOR The Master's Use

Take my life, and let it be
Consecrated, Lord, to Thee.

Take my moments and my days;
Let them flow in ceaseless praise.

Take my hands, and let them move
At the impulse of Thy love.

Take my feet, and let them be
Swift and 'beautiful' for Thee.

Take my voice, and let me sing
Always, only, for my King.

Take my lips and let them be
Filled with messages from Thee.

Take my silver and my gold;
Not a mite would I withhold.

Take my intellect, and use
Every power as Thou shalt choose.

Take my will and make it Thine;
It shall be no longer mine.

Take my heart; it is Thine own;
It shall be Thy royal throne.

Take my love; my Lord, I pour
At Thy feet its treasure-store.

Take myself, and I will be
Ever, only, ALL for Thee.

CHAPTER I
Our Lives kept for Jesus

'Keep my life, that it may be
Consecrated, Lord, to Thee.'

Many a heart has echoed the little song:

'Take my life, and let it be
Consecrated, Lord, to Thee!'

And yet those echoes have not been, in every case and at all
times, so clear, and full, and firm, so continuously glad as we
would wish, and perhaps expected. Some of us have said:

'I launch me forth upon a sea
Of boundless love and tenderness;'

and after a little we have found, or fancied, that there is a hidden leak in our barque, and though we are doubtless still afloat,
yet we are not sailing with the same free, exultant confidence as
at first. What is it that has dulled and weakened the echo of our
consecration song? what is the little leak that hinders the swift
and buoyant course of our consecrated life? Holy Father, let Thy
loving spirit guide the hand that writes, and strengthen the heart
of every one who reads what shall be written, for Jesus' sake.

While many a sorrowfully varied answer to these questions may,
and probably will, arise from touched and sensitive consciences,
each being shown by God's faithful Spirit the special sin, the special yielding to temptation which has hindered and spoiled the
blessed life which they sought to enter and enjoy, it seems to me
that one or other of two things has lain at the outset of the failure
and disappointment.

First, it may have arisen from want of the simplest belief in the
simplest fact, as well as want of trust in one of the simplest and
plainest words our gracious Master ever uttered! The unbelieved
fact being simply that He hears us; the untrusted word being one
of those plain, broad foundation-stones on which we rested our
whole weight, it may be many years ago, and which we had no idea
we ever doubted, or were in any danger of doubting now,—'Him
that cometh to Me I will in no wise cast out.'

'Take my life!' We have said it or sung it before the Lord, it may be many times; but if it were only once whispered in His ear with full purpose of heart, should we not believe that He heard it? And if we know that He heard it, should we not believe that He has answered it, and fulfilled this, our heart's desire? For with Him hearing means heeding. Then why should we doubt that He did verily take our lives when we offered them—our bodies when we presented them? Have we not been wronging His faithfulness all this time by practically, even if unconsciously, doubting whether the prayer ever really reached Him? And if so, is it any wonder that we have not realized all the power and joy of full consecration? By some means or other He has to teach us to trust implicitly at every step of the way. And so, if we did not really trust in this matter, He has had to let us find out our want of trust by withholding the sensible part of the blessing, and thus stirring us up to find out why it is withheld.

An offered gift must be either accepted or refused. Can He have refused it when He has said, 'Him that cometh to Me I will in no wise cast out'? If not, then it must have been accepted. It is just the same process as when we came to Him first of all, with the intolerable burden of our sins. There was no help for it but to come with them to Him, and take His word for it that He would not and did not cast us out. And so coming, so believing, we found rest to our souls; we found that His word was true, and that His taking away our sins was a reality.

Some give their lives to Him then and there, and go forth to live thenceforth not at all unto themselves, but unto Him who died for them. This is as it should be, for conversion and consecration ought to be simultaneous. But practically it is not very often so, except with those in whom the bringing out of darkness into marvellous light has been sudden and dazzling, and full of deepest contrasts. More frequently the work resembles the case of the Hebrew servant described in Exodus xxi., who, after six years' experience of a good master's service, dedicates himself voluntarily, unreservedly, and irrevocably to it, saying, 'I love my master; I will not go out free;' the master then accepting and sealing him to a life-long service, free in law, yet bound in love. This seems to be a figure of later consecration founded on experience and love.

And yet, as at our first coming, it is less than nothing, worse than nothing that we have to bring; for our lives, even our redeemed and pardoned lives, are not only weak and worthless, but defiled and sinful. But thanks be to God for the Altar that sanctifieth the gift, even our Lord Jesus Christ Himself! By Him we draw nigh unto God; to Him, as one with the Father, we offer our living sacrifice; in Him, as the Beloved of the Father, we know it is accepted. So, dear friends, when once He has wrought in us the desire to be altogether His own, and put into our hearts the prayer, 'Take my life,' let us go on our way rejoicing, believing that He has taken our lives, our hands, our feet, our voices, our intellects, our wills, our whole selves, to be ever, only, all for Him. Let us consider that a blessedly settled thing; not because of anything we have felt, or said, or done, but because we know that He heareth us, and because we know that He is true to His word.

But suppose our hearts do not condemn us in this matter, our disappointment may arise from another cause. It may be that we have not received, because we have not asked a fuller and further blessing. Suppose that we did believe, thankfully and surely, that the Lord heard our prayer, and that He did indeed answer and accept us, and set us apart for Himself; and yet we find that our consecration was not merely miserably incomplete, but that we have drifted back again almost to where we were before. Or suppose things are not quite so bad as that, still we have not quite all we expected; and even if we think we can truly say, 'O God, my heart is fixed,' we find that, to our daily sorrow, somehow or other the details of our conduct do not seem to be fixed, something or other is perpetually slipping through, till we get perplexed and distressed. Then we are tempted to wonder whether after all there was not some mistake about it, and the Lord did not really take us at our word, although we took Him at His word. And then the struggle with one doubt, and entanglement, and temptation only seems to land us in another. What is to be done then?

First, I think, very humbly and utterly honestly to search and try our ways before our God, or rather, as we shall soon realize our helplessness to make such a search, ask Him to do it for us, praying for His promised Spirit to show us unmistakably if there is any secret thing with us that is hindering both the inflow and outflow of His grace to us and through us. Do not let us shrink from some unexpected flash into a dark corner; do not let us wince at the sudden touching of a hidden plague-spot. The Lord always does His own work thoroughly if we will only let Him do it; if we put our case into His hands, He will search and probe fully and firmly, though very tenderly. Very painfully, it may be, but only that He may do the very thing we want,—cleanse us and heal us thoroughly, so that we may set off to walk in real newness of life. But if we do not put it unreservedly into His hands, it will be no use thinking or talking about our lives being consecrated to Him. The heart that is not entrusted to Him for searching, will not be undertaken by Him for cleansing; the life that fears to come to the light lest any deed should be reproved, can never know the blessedness and the privileges of walking in the light.

But what then? When He has graciously again put a new song in our mouth, and we are singing,

'Ransomed, healed, restored, forgiven,
Who like me His praise should sing?'

and again with fresh earnestness we are saying,

'Take my life, and let it be
Consecrated, Lord, to Thee!'

are we only to look forward to the same disappointing experience over again? are we always to stand at the threshold? Consecration is not so much a step as a course; not so much an act, as a position to which a course of action inseparably belongs. In so far as it is a course and a position, there must naturally be a definite entrance upon it, and a time, it may be a moment, when that entrance is made. That is when we say, 'Take'; but we do not want to go on taking a first step over and over again. What we want now is to be maintained in that position, and to fulfil that course. So let us go on to another prayer. Having already said, 'Take my life, for I cannot give it to Thee,' let us now say, with deepened conviction, that without Christ we really can do nothing,—'Keep my life, for I cannot keep it for Thee.'

Let us ask this with the same simple trust to which, in so many other things, He has so liberally and graciously responded. For this is the confidence that we have in Him, that if we ask anything according to His will, He heareth us; and if we know that He hears us, whatsoever we ask, we know that we have the petitions that we desired of Him. There can be no doubt that this petition is according to His will, because it is based upon many a promise. May I give it to you just as it floats through my own mind again and again, knowing whom I have believed, and being persuaded that He is able to keep that which I have committed unto Him?

Keep my life, that it may be
Consecrated, Lord, to Thee.

Keep my moments and my days;
Let them flow in ceaseless praise.

Keep my hands, that they may move
At the impulse of Thy love.

Keep my feet, that they may be
Swift and 'beautiful' for Thee.

Keep my voice, that I may sing
Always, only, for my King.

Keep my lips, that they may be
Filled with messages from Thee.

Keep my silver and my gold;
Not a mite would I withhold.

Keep my intellect, and use
Every power as Thou shalt choose.

Keep my will, oh, keep it Thine!
For it is no longer mine.

Keep my heart; it is Thine own;
It is now Thy royal throne.

Keep my love; my Lord, I pour
At Thy feet its treasure-store.

Keep myself, that I may be
Ever, only, ALL for Thee.

Yes! He who is able and willing to take unto Himself, is no less able and willing to keep for Himself. Our willing offering has been made by His enabling grace, and this our King has 'seen with joy.' And now we pray, 'Keep this for ever in the imagination of the thoughts of the heart of Thy people' (1 Chron. xxix. 17, 18).

This blessed 'taking,' once for all, which we may quietly believe as an accomplished fact, followed by the continual 'keeping,' for which He will be continually inquired of by us, seems analogous to the great washing by which we have part in Christ, and the repeated washing of the feet for which we need to be continually coming to Him. For with the deepest and sweetest consciousness that He has indeed taken our lives to be His very own, the need of His active and actual keeping of them in every detail and at every moment is most fully realized. But then we have the promise of our faithful God, 'I the Lord do keep it, I will keep it night and day.' The only question is, will we trust this promise, or will we not? If we do, we shall find it come true. If not, of course it will not be realized. For unclaimed promises are like uncashed cheques; they will keep us from bankruptcy, but not from want. But if not, why not? What right have we to pick out one of His faithful sayings, and say we don't expect Him to fulfil that? What defence can we bring, what excuse can we invent, for so doing?

If you appeal to experience against His faithfulness to His word, I will appeal to experience too, and ask you, did you ever really trust Jesus to fulfil any word of His to you, and find your trust deceived? As to the past experience of the details of your life not being kept for Jesus, look a little more closely at it, and you will find that though you may have asked, you did not trust. Whatever you did really trust Him to keep, He has kept, and the unkept things were never really entrusted. Scrutinize this past experience as you will, and it will only bear witness against your unfaithfulness, never against His absolute faithfulness.

Yet this witness must not be unheeded. We must not forget the things that are behind till they are confessed and forgiven. Let us now bring all this unsatisfactory past experience, and, most of all, the want of trust which has been the poison-spring of its course, to the precious blood of Christ, which cleanseth us, even us, from all sin, even this sin. Perhaps we never saw that we were not trusting Jesus as He deserves to be trusted; if so, let us wonderingly hate ourselves the more that we could be so trustless to such a Saviour, and so sinfully dark and stupid that we did not even see it. And oh, let us wonderingly love Him the more that He has been so patient and gentle with us, upbraiding not, though in our slow-hearted foolishness we have been grieving Him by this subtle unbelief, and then, by His grace, may we enter upon a new era of experience, our lives kept for Him more fully than ever before, because we trust Him more simply and unreservedly to keep them!

Here we must face a question, and perhaps a difficulty. Does it not almost seem as if we were at this point led to trusting to our trust, making everything hinge upon it, and thereby only removing a subtle dependence upon ourselves one step farther back, disguising instead of renouncing it? If Christ's keeping depends upon our trusting, and our continuing to trust depends upon ourselves, we are in no better or safer position than before, and shall only be landed in a fresh series of disappointments. The old story, something for the sinner to do, crops up again here, only with the ground shifted from 'works' to trust. Said a friend to me, 'I see now! I did trust Jesus to do everything else for me, but I thought that this trusting was something that I had got to do.' And so, of course, what she 'had got to do' had been a perpetual effort and frequent failure. We can no more trust and keep on trusting than we can do anything else of ourselves. Even in this it must be 'Jesus only'; we are not to look to Him only to be the Author and Finisher of our faith, but we are to look to Him for all the intermediate fulfilment of the work of faith (2 Thess. i. 11); we must ask Him to go on fulfilling it in us, committing even this to His power.

> For we both may and must
> Commit our very faith to Him,
> Entrust to him our trust.

What a long time it takes us to come down to the conviction, and still more to the realization of the fact that without Him we can do nothing, but that He must work all our works in us! This is the work of God, that ye believe in Him whom He has sent. And no less must it be the work of God that we go on believing, and that we go on trusting. Then, dear friends, who are longing to trust Him with unbroken and unwavering trust, cease the effort and drop the burden, and now entrust your trust to Him! He is just as well able to keep that as any other part of the complex lives which we want Him to take and keep for Himself. And oh, do not pass on content with the thought, 'Yes, that is a good idea; perhaps I should find that a great help!' But, 'Now, then, do it.' It is no help to the sailor to see a flash of light across a dark sea, if he does not instantly steer accordingly.

Consecration is not a religiously selfish thing. If it sinks into that, it ceases to be consecration. We want our lives kept, not that we may feel happy, and be saved the distress consequent on wandering, and get the power with God and man, and all the other privileges linked with it. We shall have all this, because the lower is included in the higher; but our true aim, if the love of Christ constraineth us, will be far beyond this. Not for 'me' at all but 'for Jesus'; not for my safety, but for His glory; not for my comfort, but for His joy; not that I may find rest, but that He may see the travail of His soul, and be satisfied! Yes, for Him I want to be kept. Kept for His sake; kept for His use; kept to be His witness; kept for His joy! Kept for Him, that in me He may show forth some tiny sparkle of His light and beauty; kept to do His will and His work in His own way; kept, it may be, to suffer for His sake; kept for Him, that He may do just what seemeth Him good with me; kept, so that no other lord shall have any more dominion over me, but that Jesus shall have all there is to have;—little enough, indeed, but not divided or diminished by any other claim. Is not this, O you who love the Lord—is not this worth living for, worth asking for, worth trusting for?

This is consecration, and I cannot tell you the blessedness of it. It is not the least use arguing with one who has had but a taste of its blessedness, and saying to him, 'How can these things be?' It is not the least use starting all sorts of difficulties and theoretical suppositions about it with such a one, any more than it was when the Jews argued with the man who said, 'One thing I know, that whereas I was blind, now I see.' The Lord Jesus does take the life that is offered to Him, and He does keep the life for Himself that is entrusted to Him; but until the life is offered we cannot know the taking, and until the life is entrusted we cannot know or understand the keeping. All we can do is to say, 'O taste and see!' and bear witness to the reality of Jesus Christ, and set to our seal that we have found Him true to His every word, and that we have proved Him able even to do exceeding abundantly above all we asked or thought. Why should we hesitate to bear this testimony? We have done nothing at all; we have, in all our efforts, only proved to ourselves, and perhaps to others, that we had no power either to give or keep our lives. Why should we not, then, glorify His grace by acknowledging that we have found Him so wonderfully and tenderly gracious and faithful in both taking and keeping as we never supposed or imagined? I shall never forget the smile and emphasis with which a poor working man bore this witness to his Lord. I said to him, 'Well, H., we have a good Master, have we not?' 'Ah,' said he, 'a deal better than ever I thought!' That summed up his experience, and so it will sum up the experience of every one who will but yield their lives wholly to the same good Master.

I cannot close this chapter without a word with those, especially my younger friends, who, although they have named the name of Christ, are saying, 'Yes, this is all very well for some people, or for older people, but I am not ready for it; I can't say I see my way to this sort of thing.' I am going to take the lowest ground for a minute, and appeal to your 'past experience.' Are you satisfied with your experience of the other 'sort of thing'? Your pleasant pursuits, your harmless recreations, your nice occupations, even your improving ones, what fruit are you having from them? Your social intercourse, your daily talks and walks, your investments of all the time that remains to you over and above the absolute duties God may have given you, what fruit that shall remain have you from all this? Day after day passes on, and year after year, and what shall the harvest be? What is even the present return?

Are you getting any real and lasting satisfaction out of it all? Are you not finding that things lose their flavour, and that you are spending your strength day after day for nought? that you are no more satisfied than you were a year ago—rather less so, if anything? Does not a sense of hollowness and weariness come over you as you go on in the same round, perpetually getting through things only to begin again? It cannot be otherwise. Over even the freshest and purest earthly fountains the Hand that never makes a mistake has written, 'He that drinketh of this water shall thirst again.' Look into your own heart and you will find a copy of that inscription already traced, 'Shall thirst again.' And the characters are being deepened with every attempt to quench the inevitable thirst and weariness in life, which can only be satisfied and rested in full consecration to God. For 'Thou hast made us for Thyself, and the heart never resteth till it findeth rest in Thee.' To-day I tell you of a brighter and happier life, whose inscription is, 'Shall never thirst,'—a life that is no dull round-and-round in a circle of unsatisfactorinesses, but a life that has found its true and entirely satisfactory centre, and set itself towards a shining and entirely satisfactory goal, whose brightness is cast over every step of the way. Will you not seek it?

Do not shrink, and suspect, and hang back from what it may involve, with selfish and unconfiding and ungenerous half-heartedness. Take the word of any who have willingly offered themselves unto the Lord, that the life of consecration is 'a deal better than they thought!' Choose this day whom you will serve with real, thorough-going, whole-hearted service, and He will receive you; and you will find, as we have found, that He is such a good Master that you are satisfied with His goodness, and that you will never want to go out free. Nay, rather take His own word for it; see what He says: 'If they obey and serve Him, they shall spend their days in prosperity, and their years in pleasures.' You cannot possibly understand that till you are really in His service! For He does not give, nor even show, His wages before you enter it. And He says, 'My servants shall sing for joy of heart.' But you cannot try over that song to see what it is like, you cannot even read one bar of it, till your nominal or even promised service is exchanged for real and undivided consecration. But when He can call you 'My servant,' then you will find yourself singing for joy of heart, because He says you shall.

'And who, then, is willing to consecrate his service this day unto the Lord?'

'Do not startle at the term, or think, because you do not understand all it may include, you are therefore not qualified for it. I dare say it comprehends a great deal more than either you or I understand, but we can both enter into the spirit of it, and the detail will unfold itself as long as our probation shall last. Christ demands a hearty consecration in will, and He will teach us what that involves in act.'

This explains the paradox that 'full consecration' may be in one sense the act of a moment, and in another the work of a lifetime. It must be complete to be real, and yet if real, it is always incomplete; a point of rest, and yet a perpetual progression.

Suppose you make over a piece of ground to another person. You give it up, then and there, entirely to that other; it is no longer in your own possession; you no longer dig and sow, plant and reap, at your discretion or for your own profit. His occupation of it is total; no other has any right to an inch of it; it is his affair thenceforth what crops to arrange for and how to make the most of it. But his practical occupation of it may not appear all at once. There may be waste land which he will take into full cultivation only by degrees, space wasted for want of draining or by over fencing, and odd corners lost for want of enclosing; fields yielding smaller returns than they might because of hedgerows too wide and shady, and trees too many and spreading, and strips of good soil trampled into uselessness for want of defined pathways.

Just so is it with our lives. The transaction of, so to speak, making them over to God is definite and complete. But then begins the practical development of consecration. And here He leads on 'softly, according as the children be able to endure.' I do not suppose any one sees anything like all that it involves at the outset. We have not a notion what an amount of waste of power there has been in our lives; we never measured out the odd corners and the undrained bits, and it never occurred to us what good fruit might be grown in our straggling hedgerows, nor how the shade of our trees has been keeping the sun from the scanty crops. And so, season by season, we shall be sometimes not a little startled, yet always very glad, as we find that bit by bit the Master shows how much more may be made of our ground, how much more He is able to make of it than we did; and we shall be willing to work under Him and do exactly what He points out, even if it comes to cutting down a shady tree, or clearing out a ditch full of pretty weeds and wild-flowers.

As the seasons pass on, it will seem as if there was always more and more to be done; the very fact that He is constantly showing us something more to be done in it, proving that it is really His ground. Only let Him have the ground, no matter how poor or overgrown the soil may be, and then 'He will make her wilderness like Eden, and her desert like the garden of the Lord.' Yes, even our 'desert'! And then we shall sing, 'My beloved has gone down into His garden, to the beds of spices, to feed in the gardens and to gather lilies.'

Made for Thyself, O God!
Made for Thy love, Thy service, Thy delight;
Made to show forth Thy wisdom, grace, and might;
Made for Thy praise, whom veiled archangels laud:
Oh, strange and glorious thought, that we may be
A joy to Thee!

Yet the heart turns away
From this grand destiny of bliss, and deems
'Twas made for its poor self, for passing dreams,
Chasing illusions melting day by day,
Till for ourselves we read on this world's best,
'This is not rest!'

CHAPTER II
Our Moments kept for Jesus

'Keep my moments and my days;
Let them flow in ceaseless praise.'

It may be a little help to writer and reader if we consider some of the practical details of the life which we desire to have 'kept for Jesus' in the order of the little hymn at the beginning of this book, with the one word 'take' changed to 'keep.' So we will take a couplet for each chapter.

The first point that naturally comes up is that which is almost synonymous with life—our time. And this brings us at once face to face with one of our past difficulties, and its probable cause.

When we take a wide sweep, we are so apt to be vague. When we are aiming at generalities we do not hit the practicalities. We forget that faithfulness to principle is only proved by faithfulness in detail. Has not this vagueness had something to do with the constant ineffectiveness of our feeble desire that our time should be devoted to God?

In things spiritual, the greater does not always include the less, but, paradoxically, the less more often includes the greater. So in this case, time is entrusted to us to be traded with for our Lord. But we cannot grasp it as a whole. We instinctively break it up ere we can deal with it for any purpose. So when a new year comes round, we commit it with special earnestness to the Lord. But as we do so, are we not conscious of a feeling that even a year is too much for us to deal with? And does not this feeling, that we are dealing with a larger thing than we can grasp, take away from the sense of reality? Thus we are brought to a more manageable measure; and as the Sunday mornings or the Monday mornings come round, we thankfully commit the opening week to Him, and the sense of help and rest is renewed and strengthened. But not even the six or seven days are close enough to our hand; even to-morrow exceeds our tiny grasp, and even to-morrow's grace is therefore not given to us. So we find the need of considering our lives as a matter of day by day, and that any more general committal and consecration of our time does not meet the case so truly. Here we have found much comfort and help, and if results have not been entirely satisfactory, they have, at least, been more so than before we reached this point of subdivision.

But if we have found help and blessing by going a certain distance in one direction, is it not probable we shall find more if we go farther in the same? And so, if we may commit the days to our Lord, why not the hours, and why not the moments? And may we not expect a fresh and special blessing in so doing?

We do not realize the importance of moments. Only let us consider those two sayings of God about them, 'In a moment shall they die,' and, 'We shall all be changed in a moment,' and we shall think less lightly of them. Eternal issues may hang upon any one of them, but it has come and gone before we can even think about it. Nothing seems less within the possibility of our own keeping, yet nothing is more inclusive of all other keeping. Therefore let us ask Him to keep them for us.

Are they not the tiny joints in the harness through which the darts of temptation pierce us? Only give us time, we think, and we should not be overcome. Only give us time, and we could pray and resist, and the devil would flee from us! But he comes all in a moment; and in a moment—an unguarded, unkept one—we utter the hasty or exaggerated word, or think the un-Christ-like thought, or feel the un-Christ-like impatience or resentment.

But even if we have gone so far as to say, 'Take my moments,' have we gone the step farther, and really let Him take them—really entrusted them to Him? It is no good saying 'take,' when we do not let go. How can another keep that which we are keeping hold of? So let us, with full trust in His power, first commit these slippery moments to Him,—put them right into His hand,—and then we may trustfully and happily say, 'Lord, keep them for me! Keep every one of the quick series as it arises. I cannot keep them for Thee; do Thou keep them for Thyself!'

But the sanctified and Christ-loving heart cannot be satisfied with only negative keeping. We do not want only to be kept from displeasing Him, but to be kept always pleasing Him. Every 'kept from' should have its corresponding and still more blessed 'kept for.' We do not want our moments to be simply kept from Satan's use, but kept for His use; we want them to be not only kept from sin, but kept for His praise.

Do you ask, 'But what use can he make of mere moments?' I will not stay to prove or illustrate the obvious truth that, as are the moments so will be the hours and the days which they build.

You understand that well enough. I will answer your question as it stands.

Look back through the history of the Church in all ages, and mark how often a great work and mighty influence grew out of a mere moment in the life of one of God's servants; a mere moment, but overshadowed and filled with the fruitful power of the Spirit of God. The moment may have been spent in uttering five words, but they have fed five thousand, or even five hundred thousand. Or it may have been lit by the flash of a thought that has shone into hearts and homes throughout the land, and kindled torches that have been borne into earth's darkest corners. The rapid speaker or the lonely thinker little guessed what use his Lord was making of that single moment. There was no room in it for even a thought of that. If that moment had not been, though perhaps unconsciously, 'kept for Jesus,' but had been otherwise occupied, what a harvest to His praise would have been missed!

The same thing is going on every day. It is generally a moment—either an opening or a culminating one—that really does the work. It is not so often a whole sermon as a single short sentence in it that wings God's arrow to a heart. It is seldom a whole conversation that is the means of bringing about the desired result, but some sudden turn of thought or word, which comes with the electric touch of God's power. Sometimes it is less than that; only a look (and what is more momentary?) has been used by Him for the pulling down of strongholds. Again, in our own quiet waiting upon God, as moment after moment glides past in the silence at His feet, the eye resting upon a page of His Word, or only looking up to Him through the darkness, have we not found that He can so irradiate one passing moment with His light that its rays never die away, but shine on and on through days and years? Are not such moments proved to have been kept for Him? And if some, why not all?

This view of moments seems to make it clearer that it is impossible to serve two masters, for it is evident that the service of a moment cannot be divided. If it is occupied in the service of self, or any other master, it is not at the Lord's disposal; He cannot make use of what is already occupied.

Oh, how much we have missed by not placing them at his disposal! What might He not have done with the moments freighted with self or loaded with emptiness, which we have carelessly let drift by! Oh, what might have been if they had all been kept for Jesus! How He might have filled them with His light and life, enriching our own lives that have been impoverished by the waste, and using them in far-spreading blessing and power!

While we have been undervaluing these fractions of eternity, what has our gracious God been doing in them? How strangely touching are the words, 'What is man, that Thou shouldest set Thine heart upon him, and that Thou shouldest visit him every morning, and try him every moment?' Terribly solemn and awful would be the thought that He has been trying us every moment, were it not for the yearning gentleness and love of the Father revealed in that wonderful expression of wonder, 'What is man, that Thou shouldest set Thine heart upon him?' Think of that ceaseless setting of His heart upon us, careless and forgetful children as we have been! And then think of those other words, none the less literally true because given under a figure: 'I, the Lord, do keep it; I will water it every moment.'

We see something of God's infinite greatness and wisdom when we try to fix our dazzled gaze on infinite space. But when we turn to the marvels of the microscope, we gain a clearer view and more definite grasp of these attributes by gazing on the perfection of His infinitesimal handiworks. Just so, while we cannot realize the infinite love which fills eternity, and the infinite vistas of the great future are 'dark with excess of light' even to the strongest telescopes of faith, we see that love magnified in the microscope of the moments, brought very close to us, and revealing its unspeakable perfection of detail to our wondering sight.

But we do not see this as long as the moments are kept in our own hands. We are like little children closing our fingers over diamonds. How can they receive and reflect the rays of light, analyzing them into all the splendour of their prismatic beauty, while they are kept shut up tight in the dirty little hands? Give them up; let our Father hold them for us, and throw His own great light upon them, and then we shall see them full of fair colours of His manifold loving-kindnesses; and let Him always keep them for us, and then we shall always see His light and His love reflected in them.

And then, surely, they shall be filled with praise. Not that we are to be always singing hymns, and using the expressions of other people's praise, any more than the saints in glory are always literally singing a new song. But praise will be the tone, the colour, the atmosphere in which they flow; none of them away from it or out of it.

Is it a little too much for them all to 'flow in ceaseless praise'?

Well, where will you stop? What proportion of your moments do you think enough for Jesus? How many for the spirit of praise, and how many for the spirit of heaviness? Be explicit about it, and come to an understanding. If He is not to have all, then how much? Calculate, balance, and apportion. You will not be able to do this in heaven—you know it will be all praise there; but you are free to halve your service of praise here, or to make the proportion what you will.

Yet,—He made you for His glory.
Yet,—He chose you that you should be to the praise of His glory.
Yet,—He loves you every moment, waters you every moment,
 watches you unslumberingly, cares for you unceasingly.
Yet,—He died for you!

Dear friends, one can hardly write it without tears. Shall you or I remember all this love, and hesitate to give all our moments up to Him? Let us entrust Him with them, and ask Him to keep them all, every single one, for His own beloved self, and fill them all with His praise, and let them all be to His praise!

Chapter III
Our Hands Kept for Jesus

'Keep my hands, that they may move
At the impulse of Thy love.'

When the Lord has said to us, 'Is thine heart right, as My heart is with thy heart?' the next word seems to be, 'If it be, give Me thine hand.'

What a call to confidence, and love, and free, loyal, happy service is this! and how different will the result of its acceptance be from the old lamentation: 'We labour and have no rest; we have given the hand to the Egyptians and to the Assyrians.' In the service of these 'other lords,' under whatever shape they have presented themselves, we shall have known something of the meaning of having 'both the hands full with travail and vexation of spirit.' How many a thing have we 'taken in hand,' as we say, which we expected to find an agreeable task, an interest in life, a something towards filling up that unconfessed 'aching void' which is often most real when least acknowledged; and after a while we have found it change under our hands into irksome travail, involving perpetual vexation of spirit! The thing may have been of the earth and for the world, and then no wonder it failed to satisfy even the instinct of work, which comes natural to many of us. Or it may have been right enough in itself, something for the good of others so far as we understood their good, and unselfish in all but unravelled motive, and yet we found it full of tangled vexations, because the hands that held it were not simply consecrated to God. Well, if so, let us bring these soiled and tangle-making hands to the Lord, 'Let us lift up our heart with our hands' to Him, asking Him to clear and cleanse them.

If He says, 'What is that in thine hand?' let us examine honestly whether it is something which He can use for His glory or not. If not, do not let us hesitate an instant about dropping it. It may be something we do not like to part with; but the Lord is able to give thee much more than this, and the first glimpse of the excellency of the knowledge of Christ Jesus your Lord will enable us to count those things loss which were gain to us.

But if it is something which He can use, He will make us do ever so much more with it than before. Moses little thought what the Lord was going to make him do with that 'rod in his hand'! The first thing he had to do with it was to 'cast it on the ground,' and see it pass through a startling change. After this he was commanded to take it up again, hard and terrifying as it was to do so. But when it became again a rod in his hand, it was no longer what it was before, the simple rod of a wandering desert shepherd. Henceforth it was 'the rod of God in his hand' (Ex. iv. 20), wherewith he should do signs, and by which God Himself would do 'marvellous things' (Ps. lxxviii. 12).

If we look at any Old Testament text about consecration, we shall see that the marginal reading of the word is, 'fill the hand' (e. g. Ex. xxviii. 41; 1 Chron. xxix. 5). Now, if our hands are full of 'other things,' they cannot be filled with 'the things that are Jesus Christ's'; there must be emptying before there can be any true filling. So if we are sorrowfully seeing that our hands have not been kept for Jesus, let us humbly begin at the beginning, and ask Him to empty them thoroughly, that He may fill them completely.

For they must be emptied. Either we come to our Lord willingly about it, letting Him unclasp their hold, and gladly dropping the glittering weights they have been carrying, or, in very love, He will have to force them open, and wrench from the reluctant grasp the 'earthly things' which are so occupying them that He cannot have His rightful use of them. There is only one other alternative, a terrible one,—to be let alone till the day comes when not a gentle Master, but the relentless king of terrors shall empty the trembling hands as our feet follow him out of the busy world into the dark valley, for 'it is certain we can carry nothing out.'

Yet the emptying and the filling are not all that has to be considered. Before the hands of the priests could be filled with the emblems of consecration, they had to be laid upon the emblem of atonement (Lev. viii. 14, etc.). That came first. 'Aaron and his sons laid their hands upon the head of the bullock for the sin-offering.' So the transference of guilt to our Substitute, typified by that act, must precede the dedication of ourselves to God.

'My faith would lay her hand
  On that dear head of Thine,
While like a penitent I stand,
  And there confess my sin.'

The blood of that Holy Substitute was shed 'to make reconciliation upon the altar.' Without that reconciliation we cannot offer and present ourselves to God; but this being made, Christ Himself presents us. And you, that were sometime alienated, and enemies in your mind by wicked works, yet now hath He reconciled in the body of His flesh through death, to present you holy and unblamable and unreprovable in His sight.

Then Moses 'brought the ram for the burnt-offering; and Aaron and his sons laid their hands upon the head of the ram, and Moses burnt the whole ram upon the altar; it was a burnt-offering for a sweet savour, and an offering made by fire unto the Lord.' Thus Christ's offering was indeed a whole one, body, soul, and spirit, each and all suffering even unto death. These atoning sufferings, accepted by God for us, are, by our own free act, accepted by us as the ground of our acceptance.

Then, reconciled and accepted, we are ready for consecration; for then 'he brought the other ram; the ram of consecration; and Aaron and his sons laid their hands upon the head of the ram.' Here we see Christ, 'who is consecrated for evermore.' We enter by faith into union with Him who said, 'For their sakes I sanctify Myself, that they also might be sanctified through the truth.'

After all this, their hands were filled with 'consecrations for a sweet savour,' so, after laying the hand of our faith upon Christ, suffering and dying for us, we are to lay that very same hand of faith, and in the very same way, upon Him as consecrated for us, to be the source and life and power of our consecration. And then our hands shall be filled with 'consecrations,' filled with Christ, and filled with all that is a sweet savour to God in Him.

'And who then is willing to fill his hand this day unto the Lord?' Do you want an added motive? Listen again: 'Fill your hands to-day to the Lord, that He may bestow upon you a blessing this day.' Not a long time hence, not even to-morrow, but 'this day.' Do you not want a blessing? Is not your answer to your Father's 'What wilt thou?' the same as Achsah's, 'Give me a blessing!' Here is His promise of just what you so want; will you not gladly fulfil His condition? A blessing shall immediately follow. He does not specify what it shall be; He waits to reveal it. You will find it such a blessing as you had not supposed could be for you—a blessing that shall verily make you rich, with no sorrow added—a blessing this day.

All that has been said about consecration applies to our literal members. Stay a minute, and look at your hand, the hand that holds this little book as you read it. See how wonderfully it is made; how perfectly fitted for what it has to do; how ingeniously connected with the brain, so as to yield that instantaneous and instinctive obedience without which its beautiful mechanism would be very little good to us! Your hand, do you say? Whether it is soft and fair with an easy life, or rough and strong with a working one, or white and weak with illness, it is the Lord Jesus Christ's. It is not your own at all; it belongs to Him. He made it, for without Him was not anything made that was made, not even your hand. And He has the added right of purchase—He has bought it that it might be one of His own instruments. We know this very well, but have we realized it? Have we really let Him have the use of these hands of ours? and have we ever simply and sincerely asked Him to keep them for His own use?

Does this mean that we are always to be doing some definitely 'religious' work, as it is called? No, but that all that we do is to be always definitely done for Him. There is a great difference. If the hands are indeed moving 'at the impulse of His love,' the simplest little duties and acts are transfigured into holy service to the Lord.

'A servant with this clause
  Makes drudgery divine;
Who sweeps a room as for Thy laws,
  Makes that and the action fine.'
  ~George Herbert.

A Christian school-girl loves Jesus; she wants to please Him all day long, and so she practices her scales carefully and conscientiously. It is at the impulse of His love that her fingers move so steadily through the otherwise tiresome exercises. Some day her Master will find a use for her music; but meanwhile it may be just as really done unto Him as if it were Mr. Sankey at his organ, swaying the hearts of thousands. The hand of a Christian lad traces his Latin verses, or his figures, or his copying. He is doing his best, because a banner has been given him that it may be displayed, not so much by talk as by continuance in well-doing. And so, for Jesus' sake, his hand moves accurately and perseveringly.

A busy wife, or daughter, or servant has a number of little manual duties to perform. If these are done slowly and leisurely, they may be got through, but there will not be time left for some little service to the poor, or some little kindness to a suffering or troubled neighbour, or for a little quiet time alone with God and His word. And so the hands move quickly, impelled by the loving desire for service or communion, kept in busy motion for Jesus' sake. Or it may be that the special aim is to give no occasion of reproach to some who are watching, but so to adorn the doctrine that those may be won by the life who will not be won by the word. Then the hands will have their share to do; they will move carefully, neatly, perhaps even elegantly, making every thing around as nice as possible, letting their intelligent touch be seen in the details of the home, and even of the dress, doing or arranging all the little things decently and in order for Jesus' sake. And so on with every duty in every position.

It may seem an odd idea, but a simple glance at one's hand, with the recollection, 'This hand is not mine; it has been given to Jesus, and it must be kept for Jesus,' may sometimes turn the scale in a doubtful matter, and be a safeguard from certain temptations. With that thought fresh in your mind as you look at your hand, can you let it take up things which, to say the very least, are not 'for Jesus'? things which evidently cannot be used, as they most certainly are not used, either for Him or by Him? Cards, for instance! Can you deliberately hold in it books of a kind which you know perfectly well, by sadly repeated experience, lead you farther from instead of nearer to Him? books which must and do fill your mind with those 'other things' which, entering in, choke the word? books which you would not care to read at all, if your heart were burning within you at the coming of His feet to bless you? Next time any temptation of this sort approaches, just look at your hand!

It was of a literal hand that our Lord Jesus spoke when He said, 'Behold, the hand of him that betrayeth Me is with Me on the table;' and, 'He that dippeth his hand with Me in the dish, the same shall betray Me.' A hand so near to Jesus, with Him on the table, touching His own hand in the dish at that hour of sweetest, and closest, and most solemn intercourse, and yet betraying Him! That same hand taking the thirty pieces of silver! What a tremendous lesson of the need of keeping for our hands! Oh that every hand that is with Him at His sacramental table, and that takes the memorial bread, may be kept from any faithless and loveless motion! And again, it was by literal 'wicked hands' that our Lord Jesus was crucified and slain. Does not the thought that human hands have been so treacherous and cruel to our beloved Lord make us wish the more fervently that our hands may be totally faithful and devoted to Him?

Danger and temptation to let the hands move at other impulses is every bit as great to those who have nothing else to do but to render direct service, and who think they are doing nothing else. Take one practical instance—our letter-writing. Have we not been tempted (and fallen before the temptation), according to our various dispositions, to let the hand that holds the pen move at the impulse to write an unkind thought of another; or to say a clever and sarcastic thing, or a slightly coloured and exaggerated thing, which will make our point more telling; or to let out a grumble or a suspicion; or to let the pen run away with us into flippant and trifling words, unworthy of our high and holy calling? Have we not drifted away from the golden reminder, 'Should he reason with unprofitable talk, and with speeches wherewith he can do no good?' Why has this been, perhaps again and again? Is it not for want of putting our hands into our dear Master's hand, and asking and trusting Him to keep them? He could have kept; He would have kept!

Whatever our work or our special temptations may be, the principle remains the same, only let us apply it for ourselves.

Perhaps one hardly needs to say that the kept hands will be very gentle hands. Quick, angry motions of the heart will sometimes force themselves into expression by the hand, though the tongue may be restrained. The very way in which we close a door or lay down a book may be a victory or a defeat, a witness to Christ's keeping or a witness that we are not truly being kept. How can we expect that God will use this member as an instrument of righteousness unto Him, if we yield it thus as an instrument of unrighteousness unto sin? Therefore let us see to it, that it is at once yielded to Him whose right it is; and let our sorrow that it should have been even for an instant desecrated to Satan's use, lead us to entrust it henceforth to our Lord, to be kept by the power of God through faith 'for the Master's use.'

For when the gentleness of Christ dwells in us, He can use the merest touch of a finger. Have we not heard of one gentle touch on a wayward shoulder being the turning-point of a life? I have known a case in which the Master made use of less than that— only the quiver of a little finger being made the means of touching a wayward heart.

What must the touch of the Master's own hand have been! One imagines it very gentle, though so full of power. Can He not communicate both the power and the gentleness? When He touched the hand of Peter's wife's mother, she arose and ministered unto them. Do you not think the hand which Jesus had just touched must have ministered very excellently? As we ask Him to 'touch our lips with living fire,' so that they may speak effectively for Him, may we not ask Him to touch our hands, that they may minister effectively, and excel in all that they find to do for Him? Then our hands shall be made strong by the hands of the Mighty God of Jacob.

It is very pleasant to feel that if our hands are indeed our Lord's, we may ask Him to guide them, and strengthen them, and teach them. I do not mean figuratively, but quite literally. In everything they do for Him (and that should be everything we ever undertake) we want to do it well—better and better. 'Seek that ye may excel.' We are too apt to think that He has given us certain natural gifts, but has nothing practically to do with the improvement of them, and leaves us to ourselves for that. Why not ask him to make these hands of ours more handy for His service, more skilful in what is indicated as the 'next thynge' they are to do? The 'kept' hands need not be clumsy hands. If the Lord taught David's hands to war and his fingers to fight, will He not teach our hands, and fingers too, to do what He would have them do?

The Spirit of God must have taught Bezaleel's hands as well as his head, for he was filled with it not only that he might devise cunning works, but also in cutting of stones and carving of timber. And when all the women that were wise-hearted did spin with their hands, the hands must have been made skilful as well as the hearts made wise to prepare the beautiful garments and curtains.

There is a very remarkable instance of the hand of the Lord, which I suppose signifies in that case the power of His Spirit, being upon the hand of a man. In 1 Chron. xxviii. 19, we read: 'All this, said David, the Lord made me understand in writing by His hand upon me, even all the works of this pattern.' This cannot well mean that the Lord gave David a miraculously written scroll, because, a few verses before, it says that he had it all by the Spirit. So what else can it mean but that as David wrote, the hand of the Lord was upon his hand, impelling him to trace, letter by letter, the right words of description for all the details of the temple that Solomon should build, with its courts and chambers, its treasuries and vessels? Have we not sometimes sat down to write, feeling perplexed and ignorant, and wishing some one were there to tell us what to say? At such a moment, whether it were a mere note for post, or a sheet for press, it is a great comfort to recollect this mighty laying of a Divine hand upon a human one, and ask for the same help from the same Lord. It is sure to be given!

And now, dear friend, what about your own hands? Are they

consecrated to the Lord who loves you? And if they are, are you trusting Him to keep them, and enjoying all that is involved in that keeping? Do let this be settled with your Master before you go on to the next chapter.

After all, this question will hinge on another, Do you love Him? If you really do, there can surely be neither hesitation about yielding them to Him, nor about entrusting them to Him to be kept. Does He love you? That is the truer way of putting it; for it is not our love to Christ, but the love of Christ to us which constraineth us. And this is the impulse of the motion and the mode of the keeping. The steam-engine does not move when the fire is not kindled, nor when it is gone out; no matter how complete the machinery and abundant the fuel, cold coals will neither set it going nor keep it working. Let us ask Him so to shed abroad His love in our hearts by the Holy Ghost which is given unto us, that it may be the perpetual and only impulse of every action of our daily life.

Chapter IV
Our Feet kept for Jesus

'Keep my feet, that they may be
Swift and beautiful for Thee.'

The figurative keeping of the feet of His saints, with the promise that when they run they shall not stumble, is a most beautiful and helpful subject. But it is quite distinct from the literal keeping for Jesus of our literal feet.

There is a certain homeliness about the idea which helps to make it very real. These very feet of ours are purchased for Christ's service by the precious drops which fell from His own torn and pierced feet upon the cross. They are to be His errand-runners. How can we let the world, the flesh, and the devil have the use of what has been purchased with such payment?

Shall 'the world' have the use of them? Shall they carry us where the world is paramount, and the Master cannot be even named, because the mention of His Name would be so obviously out of place? I know the apparent difficulties of a subject which will at once occur in connection with this, but they all vanish when our bright banner is loyally unfurled, with its motto, 'All for Jesus!' Do you honestly want your very feet to be 'kept for Jesus'? Let these simple words, 'Kept for Jesus,' ring out next time the dancing difficulty or any other difficulty of the same kind comes up, and I know what the result will be!

Shall 'the flesh' have the use of them? Shall they carry us hither and thither merely because we like to go, merely because it pleases ourselves to take this walk or pay this visit? And after all, what a failure it is! If people only would believe it, self-pleasing is always a failure in the end. Our good Master gives us a reality and fulness of pleasure in pleasing Him which we never get out of pleasing ourselves.

Shall 'the devil' have the use of them? Oh no, of course not! We start back at this, as a highly unnecessary question. Yet if Jesus has not, Satan has. For as all are serving either the Prince of Life or the prince of this world, and as no man can serve two masters, it follows that if we are not serving the one, we are serving the other. And Satan is only too glad to disguise this service under the less startling form of the world, or the still less startling one of self. All that is not 'kept for Jesus,' is left for self or the world, and therefore for Satan.

There is no fear but that our Lord will have many uses for what is kept by Him for Himself. 'How beautiful are the feet of them that bring glad tidings of good things!' That is the best use of all; and I expect the angels think those feet beautiful, even if they are cased in muddy boots or goloshes.

Once the question was asked, 'Wherefore wilt thou run, my son, seeing that thou hast no tidings ready?' So if we want to have these beautiful feet, we must have the tidings ready which they are to bear. Let us ask Him to keep our hearts so freshly full of His good news of salvation, that our mouths may speak out of their abundance. 'If the clouds be full of rain, they empty themselves upon the earth.' The 'two olive branches empty the golden oil out of themselves.' May we be so filled with the Spirit that we may thus have much to pour out for others!

Besides the great privilege of carrying water from the wells of salvation, there are plenty of cups of cold water to be carried in all directions; not to the poor only,—ministries of love are often as much needed by a rich friend. But the feet must be kept for these; they will be too tired for them if they are tired out for self-pleasing. In such services we are treading in the blessed steps of His most holy life, who 'went about doing good.'

Then there is literal errand-going,—just to fetch something that is needed for the household, or something that a tired relative wants, whether asked or unasked. Such things should come first instead of last, because these are clearly indicated as our Lord's will for us to do, by the position in which He has placed us; while what seems more direct service, may be after all not so directly apportioned by Him. 'I have to go and buy some soap,' said one with a little sigh. The sigh was waste of breath, for her feet were going to do her Lord's will for that next half-hour much more truly than if they had carried her to her well-worked district, and left the soap to take its chance.

A member of the Young Women's Christian Association wrote a few words on this subject, which, I think, will be welcome to many more than she expected them to reach:—

'May it not be a comfort to those of us who feel we have not the mental or spiritual power that others have, to notice that the living sacrifice mentioned in Rom. xii. 1 is our "bodies"? Of course, that includes the mental power, but does it not also include the loving, sympathizing glance, the kind, encouraging word, the ready errand for another, the work of our hands, opportunities for all of which come oftener in the day than for the mental power we are often tempted to envy? May we be enabled to offer willingly that which we have. For if there be first a willing mind, it is accepted according to that a man hath, and not according to that he hath not.'

If our feet are to be kept at His disposal, our eyes must be ever toward the Lord for guidance. We must look to Him for our orders where to go. Then He will be sure to give them. 'The steps of a good man are ordered by the Lord.' Very often we find that they have been so very literally ordered for us that we are quite astonished,—just as if He had not promised!

Do not smile at a very homely thought! If our feet are not our own, ought we not to take care of them for Him whose they are? Is it quite right to be reckless about 'getting wet feet,' which might be guarded against either by forethought or afterthought, when there is, at least, a risk of hindering our service thereby? Does it please the Master when even in our zeal for His work we annoy anxious friends by carelessness in little things of this kind?

May every step of our feet be more and more like those of our beloved Master. Let us continually consider Him in this, and go where He would have gone, on the errands which He would have done, 'following hard' after Him. And let us look on to the time when our feet shall stand in the gates of the heavenly Jerusalem, when holy feet shall tread the streets of the holy city; no longer pacing any lonely path, for He hath said, 'They shall walk with Me in white.'

'And He hath said, "How beautiful the feet!"
  The "feet" so weary, travel-stained, and worn—
  The "feet" that humbly, patiently have borne
The toilsome way, the pressure, and the heat.

'The "feet," not hasting on with wingèd might,
  Nor strong to trample down the opposing foe;
  So lowly, and so human, they must go
By painful steps to scale the mountain height.

'Not unto all the tuneful lips are given,
  The ready tongue, the words so strong and sweet;
  Yet all may turn, with humble, willing "feet,"
And bear to darkened souls the light from heaven.

'And fall they while the goal far distant lies,
  With scarce a word yet spoken for their Lord—
  His sweet approval He doth yet accord;
Their "feet" are beauteous in the Master's eyes.

'With weary human "feet" He, day by day,
  Once trod this earth to work His acts of love;
  And every step is chronicled above
His servants take to follow in His way.'
~Sarah Geraldina Stock.

Chapter V
Our Voices kept for Jesus

'Keep my voice, and let me sing
Always, only, for my King.'

I have wondered a little at being told by an experienced worker,
that in many cases the voice seems the last and hardest thing to
yield entirely to the King; and that many who think and say they
have consecrated all to the Lord and His service, 'revolt' when it
comes to be a question of whether they shall sing 'always, only,' for
their King. They do not mind singing a few general sacred songs,
but they do not see their way to really singing always and only
unto and for Him. They want to bargain and balance a little. They
question and argue about what proportion they may keep for self-
pleasing and company-pleasing, and how much they must 'give
up'; and who will and who won't like it; and what they 'really must
sing,' and what they 'really must not sing' at certain times and
places; and what 'won't do,' and what they 'can't very well help,'
and so on. And so when the question, 'How much owest thou unto
my Lord?' is applied to this particularly pleasant gift, it is not met
with the loyal, free-hearted, happy response, 'All! yes, all for Jesus!'

I know there are special temptations around this matter. Vain
and selfish ones—whispering how much better a certain song
suits your voice, and how much more likely to be admired. Faithless ones—suggesting doubts whether you can make the holy song
'go.' Specious ones—asking whether you ought not to please your
neighbours, and hushing up the rest of the precept, 'Let every one
of you please his neighbour for his good to edification' (Rom. xv. 2).
Cowardly ones—telling you that it is just a little too much to expect of you, and that you are not called upon to wave your banner
in people's very faces, and provoke surprise and remark, as this
might do. And so the banner is kept furled, the witness for Jesus
is not borne, and you sing for others and not for your King.

The words had passed your lips, 'Take my voice!' And yet you will
not let Him have it; you will not let Him have that which costs you
something, just because it costs you something! And yet He lent

you that pleasant voice that you might use it for Him. And yet He, in the sureness of His perpetual presence, was beside you all the while, and heard every note as you sang the songs which were, as your inmost heart knew, not for Him.

Where is your faith? Where is the consecration you have talked about? The voice has not been kept for Him, because it has not been truly and unreservedly given to Him. Will you not now say, 'Take my voice, for I had not given it to Thee; keep my voice, for I cannot keep it for Thee'?

And He will keep it! You cannot tell, till you have tried, how surely all the temptations flee when it is no longer your battle but the Lord's; nor how completely and curiously all the difficulties vanish, when you simply and trustfully go forward in the path of full consecration in this matter. You will find that the keeping is most wonderfully real. Do not expect to lay down rules and provide for every sort of contingency. If you could, you would miss the sweetness of the continual guidance in the 'kept' course. Have only one rule about it—just to look up to your Master about every single song you are asked or feel inclined to sing. If you are 'willing and obedient,' you will always meet His guiding eye. He will always keep the voice that is wholly at His disposal. Soon you will have such experience of His immediate guidance that you will be utterly satisfied with it, and only sorrowfully wonder you did not sooner thus simply lean on it.

I have just received a letter from one who has laid her special gift at the feet of the Giver, yielding her voice to Him with hearty desire that it might be kept for His use. She writes: 'I had two lessons on singing while in Germany from our Master. One was very sweet. A young girl wrote to me, that when she had heard me sing, "O come, every one that thirsteth," she went away and prayed that she might come, and she did come, too. Is not He good? The other was: I had been tempted to join the Gesang Verein in N——. I prayed to be shown whether I was right in so doing or not. I did not see my way clear, so I went. The singing was all secular. The very first night I went I caught a bad cold on my chest, which prevented me from singing again at all till Christmas. Those were better than any lessons from a singing master!' Does not this illustrate both the keeping from and the keeping for? In the latter case I believe she honestly wished to know her Lord's will,—whether the training and practice were needed for His better service with her music, and that, therefore, she might take them for His sake; or whether the concomitants and influence would be such as to hinder the

close communion with Him which she had found so precious,
and that, therefore, she was to trust Him to give her 'much more
than this.' And so, at once, He showed her unmistakeably what
He would have her not do, and gave her the sweet consciousness
that He Himself was teaching her and taking her at her word. I
know what her passionate love for music is, and how very real and
great the compensation from Him must have been which could
thus make her right down glad about what would otherwise have
been an immense disappointment. And then, as to the former of
these two 'lessons,' the song she names was one substituted when
she said, 'Take my voice,' for some which were far more effective
for her voice. But having freely chosen to sing what might glorify
the Master rather than the singer, see how, almost immediately,
He gave her a reward infinitely outweighing all the drawing-room
compliments or concert-room applause! That one consecrated
song found echoes in heaven, bringing, by its blessed result, joy
to the angels and glory to God. And the memory of that song is
immortal; it will live through ages to come, never lost, never dying
away, when the vocal triumphs of the world's greatest singers are
past and forgotten for ever. Now you who have been taking a half-
and-half course, do you get such rewards as this? You may well
envy them! But why not take the same decided course, and share
the same blessed keeping and its fullness of hidden reward?

If you only knew, dear hesitating friends, what strength and
gladness the Master gives when we loyally 'sing forth the honour of
His Name,' you would not forego it! Oh, if you only knew the difficulties it saves! For when you sing 'always and only for your King,'
you will not get much entangled by the King's enemies, Singing an
out-and-out sacred song often clears one's path at a stroke as to
many other things. If you only knew the rewards He gives—very
often then and there; the recognition that you are one of the King's
friends by some lonely and timid one; the openings which you
quite naturally gain of speaking a word for Jesus to hearts which,
without the song, would never have given you the chance of the
word! If you only knew the joy of believing that His sure promise,
'My Word shall not return unto Me void,' will be fulfilled as you
sing that word for Him! If you only tasted the solemn happiness
of knowing that you have indeed a royal audience, that the King
Himself is listening as you sing! If you only knew—and why should
you not know? Shall not the time past of your life suffice you for
the miserable, double-hearted, calculating service? Let Him have
the whole use of your voice at any cost, and see if He does not put

many a totally unexpected new song into your mouth!

I am not writing all this to great and finished singers, but to everybody who can sing at all. Those who think they have only a very small talent, are often most tempted not to trade with it for their Lord. Whether you have much or little natural voice, there is reason for its cultivation and room for its use. Place it at your Lord's disposal, and He will show you how to make the most of it for Him; for not seldom His multiplying power is brought to bear on a consecrated voice. A puzzled singing master, very famous in his profession, said to one who tried to sing for Jesus, 'Well, you have not much voice; but, mark my words, you will always beat anybody with four times your voice!' He was right, though he did not in the least know why.

A great many so-called 'sacred songs' are so plaintive and pathetic that they help to give a gloomy idea of religion. Now don't sing these; come out boldly, and sing definitely and unmistakeably for your King, and of your King, and to your King. You will soon find, and even outsiders will have to own, that it is a good thing thus to show forth His loving-kindness and His faithfulness (see Ps. xcii. 1-3).

Here I am usually met by the query, 'But what would you advise me to sing?' I can only say that I never got any practical help from asking any one but the Master Himself, and so I would advise you to do the same! He knows exactly what will best suit your voice and enable you to sing best for Him; for He made it, and gave it just the pitch and tone He pleased, so, of course, He is the best counsellor about it. Refer your question in simplest faith to Him, and I am perfectly sure you will find it answered. He will direct you, and in some way or other the Lord will provide the right songs for you to sing. That is the very best advice I can possibly give you on the subject, and you will prove it to be so if you will act upon it.

Only one thing I would add: I believe there is nothing like singing His own words. The preacher claims the promise, 'My word shall not return unto Me void,' and why should not the singer equally claim it? Why should we use His own inspired words, with faith in their power, when speaking or writing, and content ourselves with human words put into rhyme (and sometimes very feeble rhyme) for our singing?

What a vista of happy work opens out here! What is there to prevent our using this mightiest of all agencies committed to human agents, the Word, which is quick and powerful, and sharper than any two-edged sword, whenever we are asked to sing? By this means, even a young girl may be privileged to make that Word sound in the ears of many who would not listen to it otherwise. By this, the incorruptible seed may be sown in otherwise unreachable ground.

It is a remarkable fact that it is actually the easiest way thus to take the very highest ground. You will find that singing Bible words does not excite the prejudice or contempt that any other words, sufficiently decided to be worth singing, are almost sure to do. For very decency's sake, a Bible song will be listened to respectfully; and for very shame's sake, no adverse whisper will be ventured against the words in ordinary English homes. The singer is placed on a vantage-ground, certain that at least the words of the song will be outwardly respected, and the possible ground of unfriendly criticism thus narrowed to begin with.

But there is much more than this. One feels the power of His words for oneself as one sings. One loves them and rejoices in them, and what can be greater help to any singer than that? And one knows they are true, and that they cannot really return void, and what can give greater confidence than that? God may bless the singing of any words, but He must bless the singing of His own Word, if that promise means what it says!

The only real difficulty in the matter is that Scripture songs, as a rule, require a little more practice than others. Then practise them a little more! You think nothing of the trouble of learning, for instance, a sonata, which takes you many a good hour's practice before you can render it perfectly and expressively. But you shrink from a song, the accompaniment of which you cannot read off without any trouble at all. And you never think of such a thing as taking one-tenth the pains to learn that accompaniment that you took to learn that sonata! Very likely, too, you take the additional pains to learn the sonata off by heart, so that you may play it more effectively. But you do not take pains to learn your accompaniment by heart, so that you may throw all your power into the expression of the words, undistracted by reading the notes and turning over the leaves. It is far more useful to have half a dozen Scripture songs thoroughly learnt and made your own, than to have in your portfolios several dozen easy settings of sacred poetry which you get through with your eyes fixed on the notes. And every one thus thoroughly mastered makes it easier to master others.

You will say that all this refers only to drawing-room singing. So it does, primarily, but then it is the drawing-room singing which has been so little for Jesus and so much for self and society; and so much less has been said about it, and so much less done. There would not be half the complaints of the difficulty of witnessing for Christ in even professedly Christian homes and circles, if every converted singer were also a consecrated one. For nothing raises or lowers the tone of a whole evening so much as the character of the music. There are few things which show more clearly that, as a rule, a very definite step in advance is needed beyond being a believer or even a worker for Christ. Over how many grand or cottage pianos could the Irish Society's motto, 'For Jesus' sake only,' be hung, without being either a frequent reproach, or altogether inappropriate?

But what is learnt will, naturally, be sung. And oh! how many Christian parents give their daughters the advantage of singing lessons without troubling themselves in the least about what songs are learnt, provided they are not exceptionally foolish! Still more pressingly I would say, how many Christian principals, to whom young lives are entrusted at the most important time of all for training, do not give themselves the least concern about this matter! As I write, I turn aside to refer to a list of songs learnt last term by a fresh young voice which would willingly be trained for higher work. There is just one 'sacred' song in the whole long list, and even that hardly such a one as the writer of the letter above quoted would care to sing in her fervent-spirited service of Christ. All the rest are harmless and pleasing, but only suggestive of the things of earth, the things of the world that is passing away; not one that might lead upward and onward, not one that might touch a careless heart to seek first the kingdom of God, not one that might show forth the glory and praise of our King, not one that tells out His grace and love, not one that carries His comfort to His weary ones or His joy to His loving ones. She is left to find and learn such songs as best she may; those which she will sing with all the ease and force gained by good teaching of them are no help at all, but rather hindrance in anything like wish or attempt to 'sing for Jesus.'

There is not the excuse that the songs of God's kingdom, songs which waft His own words to the souls around, would not have answered the teacher's purpose as well. God has taken care of that. He has not left Himself without witness in this direction. He has given the most perfect melodies and the richest harmonies to be linked with His own words, and no singer can be trained beyond His wonderful provision in this way. I pray that even these poor words of mine may reach the consciences of some of those who have this responsibility, and lead them to be no longer unfaithful in this important matter, no longer giving this strangely divided service—training, as they profess to desire, the souls for God, and yet allowing the voices to be trained only for the world.

But we must not run away with the idea that singing sacred songs and singing for Jesus are convertible terms. I know by sorrowful personal experience that it is very possible to sing a sacred song and not sing it for Jesus. It is easier to have one's portfolio all right than one's heart, and the repertory is more easily arranged than the motives. When we have taken our side, and the difficulties of indecision are consequently swept away, we have a new set of more subtle temptations to encounter. And although the Master will keep, the servant must watch and pray; and it is through the watching and the praying that the keeping will be effectual. We have, however, rather less excuse here than even elsewhere. For we never have to sing so very suddenly that we need be taken unawares. We have to think what to sing, and perhaps find the music, and the prelude has to be played, and all this gives quite enough time for us to recollect whose we are and whom we serve, and to arouse to the watch. Quite enough, too, for quick, trustful prayer that our singing may be kept free from that wretched self-seeking or even self-consciousness, and kept entirely for Jesus. Our best and happiest singing will flow when there is a sweet, silent undercurrent of prayerful or praisefull communion with our Master all through the song. As for nervousness, I am quite sure this is the best antidote to that.

On the other hand, it is quite possible to sing for Jesus without singing a sacred song. Do not take an ell for the inch this seems to give, and run off with the idea that it does not matter after all what you sing, so that you sing in a good frame of mind! No such thing! And the admission needs very careful guarding, and must not be wrested into an excuse for looking back to the world's songs. But cases may and do arise in which it may be right to gratify a weary father, or win a wayward brother, by trying to please them with music to which they will listen when they would not listen to the songs you would rather sing. There are cases in which this may be done most truly for the Lord's sake, and clearly under His guidance.

Sometimes cases arise in which we can only say, 'Neither know we what to do, but our eyes are upon Thee.' And when we honestly say that, depend upon it we shall find the promise true, 'I will guide thee with Mine eye.' For God is faithful, who will not suffer you to be tempted above that ye are able, but will, with the temptation, also make a way (Gr. the way) to escape, that ye may be able to bear it.

I do not know why it should be so, but it certainly is a much rarer thing to find a young gentleman singing for Jesus than a young lady,—a very rare thing to find one with a cultivated voice consecrating it to the Master's use. I have met some who were not ashamed to speak for Him, to whom it never seemed even to occur to sing for Him. They would go and teach a Bible class one day, and the next they would be practising or performing just the same songs as those who care nothing for Christ and His blood-bought salvation. They had left some things behind, but they had not left any of their old songs behind. They do not seem to think that being made new creatures in Christ Jesus had anything to do with this department of their lives. Nobody could gather whether they were on the Lord's side or not, as they stood and sang their neutral songs. The banner that was displayed in the class-room was furled in the drawing-room. Now, my friends, you who have or may have far greater opportunities of displaying that banner than we womenkind, why should you be less brave and loyal than your sisters? We are weak and you are strong naturally, but recollect that want of decision always involves want of power, and compromising Christians are always weak Christians. You will never be mighty to the pulling down of strongholds while you have one foot in the enemy's camp, or on the supposed neutral ground, if such can exist (which I doubt), between the camps. You will never be a terror to the devil till you have enlisted every gift and faculty on the Lord's side. Here is a thing in which you may practically carry out the splendid motto, 'All for Jesus.' You cannot be all for Him as long as your voice is not for Him. Which shall it be? All for Him, or partly for Him? Answer that to Him whom you call Master and Lord.

When once this drawing-room question is settled, there is not much need to expatiate about other forms of singing for Jesus. As we have opportunity we shall be willing to do good with our pleasant gift in any way or place, and it is wonderful what nice opportunities He makes for us. Whether to one little sick child or to a thousand listeners, according to the powers and openings granted, we shall take our happy position among those who minister with singing (1 Chron. vi. 32). And in so far as we really do this unto the Lord, I am quite sure He gives the hundred-fold now in this present time more than all the showy songs or self-gratifying performances we may have left for His sake. As we steadily tread this part of the path of consecration, we shall find the difficulties left behind, and the real pleasantness of the way reached, and it will be a delight to say to oneself, 'I cannot sing the old songs;' and though you have thought it quite enough to say, 'With my song will I please my friends,' especially if they happen to be pleased with a mildly sacred song or two, you will strike a higher and happier, a richer and purer note, and say with David, 'With my song will I praise Him.' David said also, 'My lips shall greatly rejoice when I sing unto Thee, and my soul, which Thou hast redeemed.' And you will find that this comes true.

Singing for Jesus, our Saviour and King;
  Singing for Jesus, the Lord whom we love!
All adoration we joyously bring,
  Longing to praise as they praise Him above.

Singing for Jesus, our Master and Friend,
  Telling His love and His marvellous grace,—
Love from eternity, love to the end,
  Love for the loveless, the sinful, and base.

Singing for Jesus, and trying to win
  Many to love Him, and join in the song;
Calling the weary and wandering in,
  Rolling the chorus of gladness along.

Singing for Jesus, our Life and our Light;
  Singing for Him as we press to the mark;
Singing for Him when the morning is bright;
  Singing, still singing, for Him in the dark!

Singing for Jesus, our Shepherd and Guide;
  Singing for gladness of heart that He gives;
Singing for wonder and praise that He died;
  Singing for blessing and joy that He lives!

Singing for Jesus, oh, singing with joy;
  Thus will we praise Him, and tell out His love,
Till He shall call us to brighter employ,
  Singing for Jesus for ever above.

Chapter VI
Our Lips kept for Jesus

'Keep my lips, that they may be
Filled with messages from Thee.'

The days are past for ever when we said, 'Our lips are our own.' Now we know that they are not our own.

And yet how many of my readers often have the miserable consciousness that they have 'spoken unadvisedly with their lips'! How many pray, 'Keep the door of my lips,' when the very last thing they think of expecting is that they will be kept! They deliberately make up their minds that hasty words, or foolish words, or exaggerated words, according to their respective temptations, must and will slip out of that door, and that it can't be helped. The extent of the real meaning of their prayer was merely that not quite so many might slip out. As their faith went no farther, the answer went no farther, and so the door was not kept.

Do let us look the matter straight in the face. Either we have committed our lips to our Lord, or we have not. This question must be settled first. If not, oh, do not let another hour pass! Take them to Jesus, and ask Him to take them.

But when you have committed them to Him, it comes to this,—is He able or is He not able to keep that which you have committed to Him? If He is not able, of course you may as well give up at once, for your own experience has abundantly proved that you are not able, so there is no help for you. But if He is able—nay, thank God there is no 'if' on this side!—say, rather, as He is able, where was this inevitable necessity of perpetual failure? You have been fancying yourself virtually doomed and fated to it, and therefore you have gone on in it, while all the time His arm was not shortened that it could not save, but you have been limiting the Holy One of Israel. Honestly, now, have you trusted Him to keep your lips this day? Trust necessarily implies expectation that what we have entrusted will be kept. If you have not expected Him to keep, you have not trusted. You may have tried, and tried very hard, but you have not trusted, and therefore you have not been kept, and your lips have been the snare of your soul (Prov. xviii. 7).

Once I heard a beautiful prayer which I can never forget; it was this: 'Lord, take my lips, and speak through them; take my mind, and think through it; take my heart, and set it on fire.' And this is the way the Master keeps the lips of His servants, by so filling their hearts with His love that the outflow cannot be unloving, by so filling their thoughts that the utterance cannot be un-Christ-like. There must be filling before there can be pouring out; and if there is filling, there must be pouring out, for He hath said, 'Out of the abundance of the heart the mouth speaketh.'

But I think we should look for something more direct and definite than this. We are not all called to be the King's ambassadors, but all who have heard the messages of salvation for themselves are called to be 'the Lord's messengers,' and day by day, as He gives us opportunity, we are to deliver 'the Lord's message unto the people.' That message, as committed to Haggai, was, 'I am with you, saith the Lord.' Is there not work enough for any lifetime in unfolding and distributing that one message to His own people? Then, for those who are still far off, we have that equally full message from our Lord to give out, which He has condensed for us into the one word, 'Come!'

It is a specially sweet part of His dealings with His messengers that He always gives us the message for ourselves first. It is what He has first told us in darkness—that is, in the secrecy of our own rooms, or at least of our own hearts—that He bids us speak in light. And so the more we sit at His feet and watch to see what He has to say to ourselves, the more we shall have to tell to others. He does not send us out with sealed despatches, which we know nothing about, and with which we have no concern.

There seems a seven-fold sequence in His filling the lips of His messengers. First, they must be purified. The live coal from off the altar must be laid upon them, and He must say, 'Lo, this hath touched thy lips, and thine iniquity is taken away, and thy sin is purged.' Then He will create the fruit of them, and this seems to be the great message of peace, 'Peace to him that is far off, and to him that is near, saith the Lord; and I will heal him' (see Isa. lvii. 19). Then comes the prayer, 'O Lord, open Thou my lips,' and its sure fulfilment. For then come in the promises, 'Behold, I have put My words in thy mouth,' and, 'They shall withal be fitted in thy lips.' Then, of course, 'the lips of the righteous feed many,' for the food is the Lord's own giving. Everything leads up to praise, and so we come next to 'My mouth shall praise Thee with joyful lips, when I remember Thee.' And lest we should fancy that 'when' rather implies that it is not, or cannot be, exactly always, we find that the meditation of Jesus throws this added light upon it, 'By Him, therefore, let us offer the sacrifice of praise to God continually, that is, the fruit of our lips, giving thanks to' (margin, confessing) 'His name.'

Does it seem a coming down from the mount to glance at one of our King's commandments, which is specially needful and applicable to this matter of our lips being kept for Him? 'Watch and pray, that ye enter not into temptation.' None of His commands clash with or supersede one another. Trusting does not supersede watching; it does but complete and effectuate it. Unwatchful trust is a delusion, and untrustful watching is in vain. Therefore let us not either wilfully or carelessly enter into temptation, whether of place, or person, or topic, which has any tendency to endanger the keeping of our lips for Jesus. Let us pray that grace may be more and more poured into our lips as it was into His, so that our speech may be always with grace. May they be pure, and sweet, and lovely, even as 'His lips, like lilies, dropping sweet-smelling myrrh.'

We can hardly consider the keeping of our lips without recollecting that upon them, more than all else (though not exclusively of all else), depends that greatest of our responsibilities, our influence. We have no choice in the matter; we cannot evade or avoid it; and there is no more possibility of our limiting it, or even tracing its limits, than there is of setting a bound to the far-vibrating sound-waves, or watching their flow through the invisible air. Not one sentence that passes these lips of ours but must be an invisibly prolonged influence, not dying away into silence, but living away into the words and deeds of others. The thought would not be quite so oppressive if we could know what we have done and shall be continuing to do by what we have said. But we never can, as a matter of fact. We may trace it a little way, and get a glimpse of some results for good or evil; but we never can see any more of it than we can see of a shooting star flashing through the night with a momentary revelation of one step of its strange path. Even if the next instant plunges it into apparent annihilation as it strikes the atmosphere of the earth, we know that it is not really so, but that its mysterious material and force must be added to the complicated materials and forces with which it has come in contact, with a modifying power none the less real because it is beyond our ken. And this is not comparing a great thing with a small, but a small thing with a great. For what is material force compared with moral force? what are gases, and vapours, and elements, compared with souls and the eternity for which they are preparing?

We all know that there is influence exerted by a person's mere presence, without the utterance of a single word. We are conscious of this every day. People seem to carry an atmosphere with them, which must be breathed by those whom they approach. Some carry an atmosphere in which all unkind thoughts shrivel up and cannot grow into expression. Others carry one in which 'thoughts of Christ and things divine' never seem able to flourish. Have you not felt how a happy conversation about the things we love best is checked, or even strangled, by the entrance of one who is not in sympathy? Outsiders have not a chance of ever really knowing what delightful intercourse we have one with another about these things, because their very presence chills and changes it. On the other hand, how another person's incoming freshens and develops it and warms us all up, and seems to give us, without the least conscious effort, a sort of lift!

If even unconscious and involuntary influence is such a power, how much greater must it be when the recognized power of words is added!

It has often struck me as a matter of observation, that open profession adds force to this influence, on whichever side it weighs; and also that it has the effect of making many a word and act, which might in other hands have been as nearly neutral as anything can be, tell with by no means neutral tendency on the wrong side. The question of Eliphaz comes with great force when applied to one who desires or professes to be consecrated altogether, life and lips: 'Should he reason with unprofitable talk, and with speeches wherewith one can do no good?' There is our standard! Idle words, which might have fallen comparatively harmlessly from one who had never named the Name of Christ, may be a stumbling-block to inquirers, a sanction to thoughtless juniors, and a grief to thoughtful seniors, when they come from lips which are professing to feed many. Even intelligent talk on general subjects by such a one may be a chilling disappointment to some craving heart, which had indulged the hope of getting help, comfort, or instruction in the things of God by listening to the conversation. It may be a lost opportunity of giving and gaining no one knows how much!

How well I recollect this disappointment to myself, again and again, when a mere child! In those early seeking days I never could understand why, sometimes, a good man whom I heard preach

or speak as if he loved Christ very much, talked about all sorts of
other things when he came back from church or missionary meet-
ing. I did so wish he would have talked about the Saviour, whom
I wanted, but had not found. It would have been so much more
interesting even to the apparently thoughtless and merry little girl.
How could he help it, I wondered, if he cared for that Pearl of Great
Price as I was sure I should care for it if I could only find it! And
oh, why didn't they ever talk to me about it, instead of about my
lessons or their little girls at home? They did not know how their
conversation was observed and compared with their sermon or
speech, and how a hungry little soul went empty away from the
supper table.

The lips of younger Christians may cause, in their turn, no less
disappointment. One sorrowful lesson I can never forget; and I will
tell the story in hope that it may save others from causes of similar
regret. During a summer visit just after I had left school, a class
of girls about my own age came to me a few times for an hour's
singing. It was very pleasant indeed, and the girls were delighted
with the hymns. They listened to all I had to say about time and
expression, and not with less attention to the more shyly-ventured
remarks about the words. Sometimes I accompanied them afterwards down the avenue; and whenever I met any of them I had
smiles and plenty of kindly words for each, which they seemed to
appreciate immensely. A few years afterwards I sat by the bedside
of one of these girls—the most gifted of them all with both heart
and head. She had been led by a wonderful way, and through long
and deep suffering, into far clearer light than I enjoyed, and had
witnessed for Christ in more ways than one, and far more brightly
than I had ever done. She told me how sorrowfully and eagerly she
was seeking Jesus at the time of those singing classes. And I never
knew it, because I never asked, and she was too shy to speak first!
But she told me more, and every word was a pang to me,—how she
used to linger in the avenue on those summer evenings, longing
that I would speak to her about the Saviour; how she hoped, week
after week, that I would just stretch out a hand to help her, just
say one little word that might be God's message of peace to her,
instead of the pleasant, general remarks about the nice hymns
and tunes. And I never did! And she went on for months, I think
for years, after, without the light and gladness which it might have
been my privilege to bring to her life. God chose other means, for
the souls that He has given to Christ cannot be lost because of
the unfaithfulness of a human instrument. But she said, and the

words often ring in my ears when I am tempted to let an opportunity slip, 'Ah, Miss F., I ought to have been yours!'

Yes, it is true enough that we should show forth His praise not only with our lips, but in our lives; but with very many Christians the other side of the prayer wants praying—they want rousing up even to wish to show it forth not only in their lives but with their lips. I wonder how many, even of those who read this, really pray, 'O Lord, open Thou my lips, and my mouth shall show forth Thy praise.'

And when opened, oh, how much one does want to have them so kept for Jesus that He may be free to make the most of them, not letting them render second-rate and indirect service when they might be doing direct and first-rate service to His cause and kingdom! It is terrible how much less is done for Him than might be done, in consequence of the specious notion that if what we are doing or saying is not bad, we are doing good in a certain way, and therefore may be quite easy about it. We should think a man rather foolish if he went on doing work which earned five shillings a week, when he might just as well do work in the same establishment and under the same master which would bring him in five pounds a week. But we should pronounce him shamefully dishonest and dishonourable if he accepted such handsome wages as the five pounds, and yet chose to do work worth only five shillings, excusing himself by saying that it was work all the same, and somebody had better do it. Do we not act something like this when we take the lower standard, and spend our strength in just making ourselves agreeable and pleasant, creating a general good impression in favour of religion, showing that we can be all things to all men, and that one who is supposed to be a citizen of the other world can be very well up in all that concerns this world? This may be good, but is there nothing better? What does it profit if we do make this favourable impression on an outsider, if we go no farther and do not use the influence gained to bring him right inside the fold, inside the only ark of safety? People are not converted by this sort of work; at any rate, I never met or heard of any one. 'He thinks it better for his quiet influence to tell!' said an affectionately excusing relative of one who had plenty of special opportunities of soul-winning, if he had only used his lips as well as his life for his Master. 'And how many souls have been converted to God by his "quiet influence" all these years?' was my reply. And to that there was no answer! For the silent shining was all very beautiful in theory, but not one of the many souls placed specially under his

influence had been known to be brought out of darkness into marvellous light. If they had, they must have been known, for such
light can't help being seen.

When one has even a glimmer of the tremendous difference between having Christ and being without Christ; when one gets but
one shuddering glimpse of what eternity is, and of what it must
mean, as well as what it may mean, without Christ; when one
gets but a flash of realization of the tremendous fact that all these
neighbours of ours, rich and poor alike, will have to spend that
eternity either with Him or without Him,—it is hard, very hard
indeed, to understand how a man or woman can believe these
things at all, and make no effort for anything beyond the tempo-
ral elevation of those around, sometimes not even beyond their
amusements! 'People must have entertainment,' they urge. I do
not find that must in the Bible, but I do find, 'We must all stand
before the judgment-seat of Christ.' And if you have any sort of
belief in that, how can you care to use those lips of yours, which
might be a fountain of life to the dying souls before you, merely
to 'entertain' them at your penny reading or other entertainment?
As you sow, so you reap. The amusing paper is read, or the lively
ballad recited, or the popular song sung, and you reap your harvest of laughter or applause, and of complacence at your success
in 'entertaining' the people. And there it ends, when you might
have sown words from which you and they should reap fruit unto
life eternal. Is this worthy work for one who has been bought with
such a price that he must say,

'Love so amazing, so divine,
Demands my soul, my life, my all'?

So far from yielding 'all' to that rightful demand of amazing love,
he does not even yield the fruit of his lips to it, much less the lips
themselves. I cannot refrain from adding, that even this lower aim
of 'entertaining' is by no means so appreciated as is supposed.
As a cottager of no more than average sense and intelligence re-
marked, 'It was all so trifling at the reading; I wish gentlefolks
would believe that poor people like something better than what's
just to make them laugh.' After all, nothing really pays like direct,
straightforward, uncompromising words about God and His works
and word. Nothing else ever made a man say, as a poor Irishman
did when he heard the Good News for the first time, 'Thank ye, sir;
you've taken the hunger off us to-day!'

Jephthah uttered all his words before the Lord; what about ours?

Well, they are all uttered before the Lord in one sense, whether we will or no; for there is not a word in my tongue, but lo, Thou, O Lord, knowest it altogether! How solemn is this thought, but how sweet does it become when our words are uttered consciously before the Lord as we walk in the light of His perpetual presence! Oh that we may so walk, that we may so speak, with kept feet and kept lips, trustfully praying, 'Let the meditation of my heart and the words of my mouth be alway acceptable in Thy sight, O Lord, my Strength and my Redeemer!'

Bearing in mind that it is not only the words which pass their lightly-hinged portal, but our literal lips which are to be kept for Jesus, it cannot be out of place, before closing this chapter, to suggest that they open both ways. What passes in should surely be considered as well as what passes out. And very many of us are beginning to see that the command, 'Whether ye eat or drink, or whatsoever ye do, do all to the glory of God,' is not fully obeyed when we drink, merely because we like it, what is the very greatest obstacle to that glory in this realm of England. What matter that we prefer taking it in a more refined form, if the thing itself is daily and actively and mightily working misery, and crime, and death, and destruction to thousands, till the cry thereof seems as if it must pierce the very heavens! And so it does—sooner, a great deal, than it pierces the walls of our comfortable dining-room! I only say here, you who have said, 'Take my lips,' stop and repeat that prayer next time you put that to your lips which is binding men and women hand and foot, and delivering them over, helpless, to Satan! Let those words pass once more from your heart out through your lips, and I do not think you will feel comfortable in letting the means of such infernal work pass in through them.

Chapter VII
Our Silver and Gold Kept for Jesus

'Keep my silver and my gold;
Not a mite would I withhold.'

'The silver and the gold is Mine, saith the Lord of Hosts.' Yes, every coin we have is literally our 'Lord's money.' Simple belief of this fact is the stepping-stone to full consecration of what He has given us, whether much or little.

'Then you mean to say we are never to spend anything on ourselves?' Not so. Another fact must be considered,—the fact that our Lord has given us our bodies as a special personal charge, and that we are responsible for keeping these bodies, according to the means given and the work required, in working order for Him. This is part of our 'own work.' A master entrusts a workman with a delicate machine, with which his appointed work is to be done. He also provides him with a sum of money with which he is to procure all that may be necessary for keeping the machine in thorough repair. Is it not obvious that it is the man's distinct duty to see to this faithfully? Would he not be failing in duty if he chose to spend it all on something for somebody else's work, or on a present for his master, fancying that would please him better, while the machine is creaking and wearing for want of a little oil, or working badly for want of a new band or screw? Just so, we are to spend what is really needful on ourselves, because it is our charge to do so; but not for ourselves, because we are not our own, but our Master's. He who knoweth our frame, knows its needs of rest and medicine, food and clothing; and the procuring of these for our own entrusted bodies should be done just as much 'for Jesus' as the greater pleasure of procuring them for some one else. Therefore there need be no quibbling over the assertion that consecration is not real and complete while we are looking upon a single shilling as our own to do what we like with. Also the principle is exactly the same, whether we are spending pence or pounds; it is our Lord's money, and must not be spent without reference to Him.

When we have asked Him to take, and continually trust Him to keep our money, 'shopping' becomes a different thing. We look up to our Lord for guidance to lay out His money prudently and rightly, and as He would have us lay it out. The gift or garment is selected consciously under His eye, and with conscious reference to Him as our own dear Master, for whose sake we shall give it, or in whose service we shall wear it, and whose own silver or gold we shall pay for it, and then it is all right.

But have you found out that it is one of the secrets of the Lord, that when any of His dear children turn aside a little bit after having once entered the blessed path of true and conscious consecration, He is sure to send them some little punishment? He will not let us go back without a sharp, even if quite secret, reminder. Go and spend ever such a little without reference to Him after you have once pledged the silver and gold entirely to Him, and see if you are not in some way rebuked for it! Very often by being permitted to find that you have made a mistake in your purchase, or that in some way it does not prosper. If you 'observe these things,' you will find that the more closely we are walking with our Lord, the more immediate and unmistakeable will be His gracious rebukes when we swerve in any detail of the full consecration to which He has called us. And if you have already experienced and recognized this part of His personal dealing with us, you will know also how we love and bless Him for it.

There is always a danger that just because we say 'all,' we may practically fall shorter than if we had only said 'some,' but said it very definitely. God recognizes this, and provides against it in many departments. For instance, though our time is to be 'all' for Him, yet He solemnly sets apart the one day in seven which is to be specially for Him. Those who think they know better than God, and profess that every day is a Sabbath, little know what floodgates of temptation they are opening by being so very wise above what is written. God knows best, and that should be quite enough for every loyal heart. So, as to money, though we place it all at our Lord's disposal, and rejoice to spend it all for Him directly or indirectly, yet I am quite certain it is a great help and safeguard, and, what is more, a matter of simple obedience to the spirit of His commands, to set aside a definite and regular proportion of our income or receipts for His direct service. It is a great mistake to suppose that the law of giving the tenth to God is merely Levitical. 'Search and look' for yourselves, and you will find that it is, like the Sabbath, a far older rule, running all through the Bible,[1] and endorsed, not abrogated, by Christ Himself. For, speaking of tithes, He said, 'These ought ye to have done, and not to leave the other undone.' To dedicate the tenth of whatever we have is mere duty; charity begins beyond it; free-will offerings and thank-offerings beyond that again.

First-fruits, also, should be thus specially set apart. This, too, we find running all through the Bible. There is a tacit appeal to our gratitude in the suggestion of them,—the very word implies bounty received and bounty in prospect. Bringing 'the first of the first-fruits into the house of the Lord thy God,' was like 'saying grace' for all the plenty He was going to bestow on the faithful Israelite. Something of gladness, too, seems always implied. 'The day of the first-fruits' was to be a day of rejoicing (compare Num. xxviii. 26 with Deut. xvi. 10, 11). There is also an appeal to loyalty: we are commanded to honour the Lord with the first-fruits of all our increase. And that is the way to prosper, for the next word is, 'So shall thy barns be filled with plenty.' The friend who first called my attention to this command, said that the setting apart first-fruits—making a proportion for God's work a first charge upon the income—always seemed to bring a blessing on the rest, and that since this had been systematically done, it actually seemed to go farther than when not thus lessened.

Presenting our first-fruits should be a peculiarly delightful act, as they are themselves the emblem of our consecrated relationship to God. For of His own will begat He us by the word of truth, that we should be a kind of first-fruits of His creatures. How sweet and hallowed and richly emblematic our little acts of obedience in this matter become, when we throw this light upon them! And how blessedly they may remind us of the heavenly company, singing, as it were, a new song before the throne; for they are the first-fruits unto God and to the Lamb.

Perhaps we shall find no better plan of detailed and systematic setting apart than the New Testament one: 'Upon the first day of the week let every one of you lay by him in store, as God hath prospered him.' The very act of literally fulfilling this apostolic command seems to bring a blessing with it, as all simple obedience does. I wish, dear friends, you would try it! You will find it a sweet reminder on His own day of this part of your consecration. You will find it an immense help in making the most of your little charities. The regular inflow will guide the outflow, and ensure your always having something for any sudden call for your Master's poor or your Master's cause. Do not say you are 'afraid you could not keep to it.' What has a consecrated life to do with being 'afraid'?

Some of us could tell of such sweet and singular lessons of trust in this matter, that they are written in golden letters of love on our memories. Of course there will be trials of our faith in this, as well as in everything else. But every trial of our faith is but a trial of His faithfulness, and is 'much more precious than gold which perisheth.'

'What about self-denial?' some reader will say. Consecration does not supersede this, but transfigures it. Literally, a consecrated life is and must be a life of denial of self. But all the effort and pain of it is changed into very delight. We love our Master; we know, surely and absolutely, that He is listening and watching our every word and way, and that He has called us to the privilege of walking 'worthy of the Lord unto all pleasing.' And in so far as this is a reality to us, the identical things which are still self-denial in one sense, become actual self-delight in another. It may be self-denial to us to turn away from something within reach of our purse which it would be very convenient or pleasant to possess. But if the Master lifted the veil, and revealed Himself standing at our side, and let us hear His audible voice asking us to reserve the price of it for His treasury, should we talk about self-denial then? Should we not be utterly ashamed to think of it? or rather, should we, for one instant, think about self or self-denial at all? Would it not be an unimaginable joy to do what He asked us to do with that money? But as long as His own unchangeable promise stands written in His word for us, 'Lo, I am with you always,' we may be sure that He is with us, and that His eye is as certainly on our opened or half-opened purse as it was on the treasury, when He sat over against it and saw the two mites cast in. So let us do our shopping 'as seeing Him who is invisible.'

It is important to remember that there is no much or little in God's sight, except as relatively to our means and willingness. 'For if there be first a willing mind, it is accepted according to that a man hath, and not according to that he hath not.' He knows what we have not, as well as what we have. He knows all about the low wages in one sphere, and the small allowance, or the fixed income with rising prices in another. And it is not a question of paying to God what can be screwed out of these, but of giving Him all, and then holding all at His disposal, and taking His orders about the disposal of all.

But I do not see at all how self-indulgence and needless extravagance can possibly co-exist with true consecration. If we really never do go without anything for the Lord's sake, but, just because

He has graciously given us means, always supply for ourselves not only every need but 'every notion,' I think it is high time we looked into the matter before God. Why should only those who have limited means have the privilege of offering to their Lord that which has really cost them something to offer? Observe, it is not merely going without something we would naturally like to have or do, but going without it for Jesus' sake. Not, 'I will go without it, because, after all, I can't very well afford it;' or, 'because I really ought to subscribe to so and so;' or, 'because I daresay I shall be glad I have not spent the money:' but, 'I will do without it, because I do want to do a little more for Him who so loves me—just that much more than I could do if I did this other thing.' I fancy this is more often the heart language of those who have to cut and contrive, than of those who are able to give liberally without any cutting and contriving at all. The very abundance of God's good gifts too often hinders from the privilege and delight of really doing without something superfluous or comfortable or usual, that they may give just that much more to their Lord. What a pity!

The following quotation may (I hope it will), touch some conscience:—'A gentleman once told us that his wine bill was £100 a year—more than enough to keep a Scripture reader always at work in some populous district. And it is one of the countless advantages of total abstinence that it at once sets free a certain amount of money for such work. Smoking, too, is a habit not only injurious to the health in a vast majority of cases, and, to our mind, very unbecoming in a "temple of the Holy Ghost," but also one which squanders money which might be used for the Lord. Expenses in dress might in most people be curtailed; expensive tastes should be denied; and simplicity in all habits of life should be a mark of the followers of Him who had not where to lay His head.'

And again: 'The self-indulgence of wealthy Christians, who might largely support the Lord's work with what they lavish upon their houses, their tables, or their personal expenditure, is very sad to see.'[2]

Here the question of jewelry seems to come in. Perhaps it was an instance of the gradual showing of the details of consecration, illustrated on page 21, but I will confess that when I wrote 'Take my silver and my gold,' it never dawned on me that anything was included beyond the coin of the realm! But the Lord 'leads on softly,' and a good many of us have been shown some capital bits of unenclosed but easily enclosable ground, which have yielded 'pleasant

fruit.' Yes, very pleasant fruit! It is wonderfully nice to light upon
something that we really never thought of as a possible gift to our
Lord, and just to give it, straight away, to Him. I do not press the
matter, but I do ask my lady friends to give it fair and candid and
prayerful consideration. Which do you really care most about—
a diamond on your finger, or a star in the Redeemer's kingdom,
shining for ever and ever? That is what it comes to, and there I
leave it.

On the other hand, it is very possible to be fairly faithful in much,
and yet unfaithful in that which is least. We may have thought
about our gold and silver, and yet have been altogether thoughtless about our rubbish! Some have a habit of hoarding away old
garments, 'pieces,' remnants, and odds and ends generally, under
the idea that they 'will come in useful some day;' very likely setting
it up as a kind of mild virtue, backed by that noxious old saying,
'Keep it by you seven years, and you'll find a use for it.' And so the
shabby things get shabbier, and moth and dust doth corrupt, and
the drawers and places get choked and crowded; and meanwhile
all this that is sheer rubbish to you might be made useful at once,
to a degree beyond what you would guess, to some poor person.

It would be a nice variety for the clever fingers of a lady's maid
to be set to work to do up old things; or some tidy woman may
be found in almost every locality who knows how to contrive children's things out of what seems to you only fit for the rag-bag,
either for her own little ones or those of her neighbours.

My sister trimmed 70 or 80 hats every spring for several years
with the contents of friends' rubbish drawers, thus relieving doz-
ens of poor mothers who liked their children to 'go tidy on Sunday,' and also keeping down finery in her Sunday school. Those
who literally fulfilled her request for 'rubbish' used to marvel at
the results.

Little scraps of carpet, torn old curtains, faded blinds, and all
such gear, go a wonderfully long way towards making poor cottag-
ers and old or sick people comfortable. I never saw anything in this
'rubbish' line yet that could not be turned to good account somehow, with a little considering of the poor and their discomforts.

I wish my lady reader would just leave this book now, and go
straight up-stairs and have a good rummage at once, and see what
can be thus cleared out. If she does not know the right recipients
at first hand, let her send it off to the nearest working clergyman's
wife, and see how gratefully it will be received! For it is a great
trial to workers among the poor not to be able to supply the needs

they see. Such supplies are far more useful than treble their small money value.

Just a word of earnest pleading for needs, closely veiled, but very sore, which might be wonderfully lightened if this wardrobe over-hauling were systematic and faithful. There are hundreds of poor clergymen's families to whom a few old garments or any house-hold oddments are as great a charity as to any of the poor under their charge. There are two Societies for aiding these with such gifts, under initials which are explained in the Reports; the P.P.C. Society—Secretary, Miss Breay, Battenhall Place, Worcester; and the A.F.D. Society—Secretary, Miss Hinton, 4 York Place, Clifton. I only ask my lady friends to send for a report to either of these devoted secretaries; and if their hearts are not so touched by the cases of brave and bitter need that they go forthwith to wardrobes and drawers to see what can be spared and sent, they are colder and harder than I give Englishwomen credit for.

There is no bondage in consecration. The two things are oppo-sites, and cannot co-exist, much less mingle. We should suspect our consecration, and come afresh to our great Counsellor about it, directly we have any sense of bondage. As long as we have an unacknowledged feeling of fidget about our account-book, and a smothered wondering what and how much we 'ought' to give, and a hushed-up wishing the thing had not been put quite so strongly before us, depend upon it we have not said unreservedly, 'Take my silver and my gold.' And how can the Lord keep what He has not been sincerely asked to take?

Ah! if we had stood at the foot of the Cross, and watched the tremendous payment of our redemption with the precious blood of Christ,—if we had seen that awful price told out, drop by drop, from His own dear patient brow and torn hands and feet, till it was ALL paid, and the central word of eternity was uttered, 'It is finished!' should we not have been ready to say, 'Not a mite will I withhold!'

My Jewels

'Shall I hold them back—my jewels?
Time has travelled many a day
Since I laid them by for ever,
Safely locking them away;
And I thought them yielded wholly.
When I dared no longer wear
Gems contrasting, oh, so sadly!

With the adorning I would bear.

'Shall I keep them still—my jewels?
  Shall I, can I yet withhold
From that living, loving Saviour
  Aught of silver or of gold?
Gold so needed, that His gospel
  May resound from sea to sea;
Can I know Christ's service lacketh,
  Yet forget His "unto Me"!

'No; I lay them down—my jewels,
  Truly on the altar now.
Stay! I see a vision passing
  Of a gem-encircled brow:
Heavenly treasure worn by Jesus,
  Souls won through my gift outpoured;
Freely, gladly I will offer
  Jewels thus to crown my Lord!'
      ~From Woman's Work.

[1] See Gen. xiv. 20, xxviii. 22; Lev. xxvii. 30, 32; Num. xviii. 21; Deut. xiv. 22; 2 Chron. xxxi. 5, 6, 12; Neh. x. 37, xii. 44, xiii. 12; Mal. iii. 8, 10; Matt. xxiii. 23; Luke xi. 42; 1 Cor xvi. 2; Heb. vii. 8.

[2] Christian Progress, vol. iii. pp. 25, 26.

Chapter VIII
Our Intellects kept for Jesus

'Keep my intellect, and use
Every power as Thou shalt choose.'

There are two distinct sets of temptations which assail those
who have, or think they have, rather less, and those who have, or
think they have, rather more than an average share of intellect;
while those who have neither less nor more are generally open in
some degree to both. The refuge and very present help from both
is the same. The intellect, whether great or small, which is committed to the Lord's keeping, will be kept and will be used by Him.

The former class are tempted to think themselves excused from
effort to cultivate and use their small intellectual gifts; to suppose
they cannot or need not seek to win souls, because they are not so
clever and apt in speech as So-and-so; to attribute to want of gift
what is really want of grace; to hide the one talent because it is not
five. Let me throw out a thought or two for these.

Which is greatest, gifts or grace? Gifts are given 'to every man according to his several ability.' That is, we have just as much given
as God knows we are able to use, and what He knows we can best
use for Him. 'But unto every one of us is given grace according to
the measure of the gift of Christ.' Claiming and using that royal
measure of grace, you may, and can, and will do more for God
than the mightiest intellect in the world without it. For which,
in the clear light of His Word, is likely to be most effectual, the
natural ability which at its best and fullest, without Christ, 'can
do nothing' (observe and believe that word!), or the grace of our
Almighty God and the power of the Holy Ghost, which is as free to
you as it ever was to any one?

If you are responsible for making use of your limited gift, are
you not equally responsible for making use of the grace and power
which are to be had for the asking, which are already yours in
Christ, and which are not limited?

Also, do you not see that when there are great natural gifts,
people give the credit to them, instead of to the grace which alone
did the real work, and thus God is defrauded of the glory? So that,

to say it reverently, God can get more glory out of a feeble instrument, because then it is more obvious that the excellency of the power is of God and not of us. Will you not henceforth say, 'Most gladly, therefore, will I rather glory in my infirmities, that the power of Christ may rest upon me'?

Don't you really believe that the Holy Spirit is just as able to draw a soul to Jesus, if He will, by your whisper of the one word, 'Come,' as by an eloquent sermon an hour long? I do! At the same time, as it is evidently God's way to work through these intellects of ours, we have no more right to expect Him to use a mind which we are wilfully neglecting, and taking no pains whatever to fit for His use, than I should have to expect you to write a beautiful inscription with my pen, if I would not take the trouble to wipe it and mend it.

The latter class are tempted to rely on their natural gifts, and to act and speak in their own strength; to go on too fast, without really looking up at every step, and for every word; to spend their Lord's time in polishing up their intellects, nominally for the sake of influence and power, and so forth, while really, down at the bottom, it is for the sake of the keen enjoyment of the process; and perhaps, most of all, to spend the strength of these intellects 'for that which doth not profit,' in yielding to the specious snare of reading clever books 'on both sides,' and eating deliberately of the tree of the knowledge of good and evil.

The mere mention of these temptations should be sufficient appeal to conscience. If consecration is to be a reality anywhere, should it not be in the very thing which you own as an extra gift from God, and which is evidently closest, so to speak, to His direct action, spirit upon spirit? And if the very strength of your intellect has been your weakness, will you not entreat Him to keep it henceforth really and entirely for Himself? It is so good of Him to have given you something to lay at His feet; shall not this goodness lead you to lay it all there, and never hanker after taking it back for yourself or the world? Do you not feel that in very proportion to the gift you need the special keeping of it? He may lead you by a way you know not in the matter; very likely He will show you that you must be willing to be a fool for His sake first, before He will condescend to use you much for His glory. Will you look up into His face and say, 'Not willing'?

He who made every power can use every power—memory, judgment, imagination, quickness of apprehension or insight; specialties of musical, poetical, oratorical, or artistic faculty; special tastes for reasoning, philosophy, history, natural science, or natural history,—all these may be dedicated to Him, sanctified by Him, and used by Him. Whatever He has given, He will use, if we will let Him. Often, in the most unexpected ways, and at the most unexpected turns, something read or acquired long ago suddenly comes into use. We cannot foresee what will thus 'come in useful'; but He knew, when He guided us to learn it, what it would be wanted for in His service. So may we not ask Him to bring His perfect foreknowledge to bear on all our mental training and storing? to guide us to read or study exactly what He knows there will be use for in the work to which He has called or will call us?

Nothing is more practically perplexing to a young Christian, whose preparation time is not quite over, or perhaps painfully limited, than to know what is most worth studying, what is really the best investment of the golden hours, while yet the time is not come for the field of active work to be fully entered, and the 'thoroughly furnishing' of the mind is the evident path of present duty. Is not His name called 'Counsellor'? and will He not be faithful to the promise of His name in this, as well as in all else?

The same applies to every subsequent stage. Only let us be perfectly clear about the principle that our intellect is not our own, either to cultivate, or to use, or to enjoy, and that Jesus Christ is our real and ever-present Counsellor, and then there will be no more worry about what to read and how much to read, and whether to keep up one's accomplishments, or one's languages, or one's 'ologies'! If the Master has need of them, He will show us; and if He has not, what need have we of them? If we go forward without His leading, we may throw away some talent, or let it get too rusty for use, which would have been most valuable when other circumstances arose or different work was given. We must not think that 'keeping' means not using at all! What we want is to have all our powers kept for His use.

In this they will probably find far higher development than in any other sort of use. I know cases in which the effect of real consecration on mere mental development has been obvious and surprising to all around. Yet it is only a confirmation of what I believe to be a great principle, viz. that the Lord makes the most of whatever is unreservedly surrendered to Him. There will always be plenty of waste in what we try to cut out for ourselves. But He wastes no material!

Chapter IX
Our Wills kept for Jesus

'Keep my will, oh, keep it Thine,
For it is no longer mine.'

Perhaps there is no point in which expectation has been so limited by experience as this. We believe God is able to do for us just so much as He has already done, and no more. We take it for granted a line must be drawn somewhere; and so we choose to draw it where experience ends, and faith would have to begin. Even if we have trusted and proved Him as to keeping our members and our minds, faith fails when we would go deeper and say, 'Keep my will!' And yet the only reason we have to give is, that though we have asked Him to take our will, we do not exactly find that it is altogether His, but that self-will crops up again and again. And whatever flaw there might be in this argument, we think the matter is quite settled by the fact that some whom we rightly esteem, and who are far better than ourselves, have the same experience, and do not even seem to think it right to hope for anything better. That is conclusive! And the result of this, as of every other faithless conclusion, is either discouragement and depression, or, still worse, acquiescence in an unyielded will, as something that can't be helped.

Now let us turn from our thoughts to God's thoughts. Verily, they are not as ours! He says He is able to do exceeding abundantly above all that we ask or think. Apply this here. We ask Him to take our wills and make them His. Does He or does He not mean what He says? and if He does, should we not trust Him to do this thing that we have asked and longed for, and not less but more? 'Is anything too hard for the Lord?' 'Hath He said, and shall He not do it?' and if He gives us faith to believe that we have the petition that we desired of Him, and with it the unspeakable rest of leaning our will wholly upon His love, what ground have we for imagining that this is necessarily to be a mere fleeting shadow, which is hardly to last an hour, but is necessarily to be exhausted ere the next breath of trial or temptation comes? Does He mock our longing by acting as I have seen an older person act to a child, by accepting some trifling gift of no intrinsic value, just to please the little one, and then throwing it away as soon as the child's attention is diverted? Is not the taking rather the pledge of the keeping, if we will but entrust Him fearlessly with it? We give Him no opportunity, so to speak, of proving His faithfulness to this great promise, because we will not fulfil the condition of reception, believing it. But we readily enough believe instead all that we hear of the unsatisfactory experience of others! Or, start from another word. Job said, 'I know that Thou canst do everything,' and we turn round and say, 'Oh yes, everything except keeping my will!' Dare we add, 'And I know that Thou canst not do that'? Yet that is what is said every day, only in other words; and if not said aloud, it is said in faithless hearts, and God hears it. What does 'Almighty' mean, if it does not mean, as we teach our little children, 'able to do everything'?

We have asked this great thing many a time, without, perhaps, realizing how great a petition we were singing, in the old morning hymn, 'Guard my first springs of thought and will!' That goes to the root of the matter, only it implies that the will has been already surrendered to Him, that it may be wholly kept and guarded.

It may be that we have not sufficiently realized the sin of the only alternative. Our wills belong either to self or to God. It may seem a small and rather excusable sin in man's sight to be self-willed, but see in what a category of iniquity God puts it! (2 Pet. ii. 10). And certainly we are without excuse when we have such a promise to go upon as, 'It is God that worketh in you both to will and to do of His pleasure.' How splendidly this meets our very deepest helplessness,—'worketh in you to will!' Oh, let us pray for ourselves and for each other, that we may know 'what is the exceeding greatness of His power to us who believe.' It does not say, 'to us who fear and doubt;' for if we will not believe, neither shall we be established. If we will not believe what God says He can do, we shall see it with our eyes, but we shall not eat thereof. 'They could not enter in because of unbelief.'

It is most comforting to remember that the grand promise, 'Thy people shall be willing in the day of Thy power,' is made by the Father to Christ Himself. The Lord Jesus holds this promise, and God will fulfil it to Him. He will make us willing because He has promised Jesus that He will do so. And what is being made willing, but having our will taken and kept?

All true surrender of the will is based upon love and knowledge of, and confidence in, the one to whom it is surrendered. We have the human analogy so often before our eyes, that it is the more strange we should be so slow to own even the possibility of it as to God. Is it thought anything so very extraordinary and high-flown,

when a bride deliberately prefers wearing a colour which was not
her own taste or choice, because her husband likes to see her in
it? Is it very unnatural that it is no distress to her to do what he
asks her to do, or to go with him where he asks her to come, even
without question or explanation, instead of doing what or going
where she would undoubtedly have preferred if she did not know
and love him? Is it very surprising if this lasts beyond the wedding
day, and if year after year she still finds it her greatest pleasure
to please him, quite irrespective of what used to be her own ways
and likings? Yet in this case she is not helped by any promise or
power on his part to make her wish what he wishes. But He who
so wonderfully condescends to call Himself the Bridegroom of His
church, and who claims our fullest love and trust, has promised
and has power to work in us to will. Shall we not claim His promise and rely on His mighty power, and say, not self-confidently,
but looking only unto Jesus—

'Keep my will, for it is Thine;
It shall be no longer mine!'

Only in proportion as our own will is surrendered, are we able to
discern the splendour of God's will.

For oh! it is a splendour,
  A glow of majesty,
A mystery of beauty
  If we will only see;
A very cloud of glory
  Enfolding you and me.

A splendour that is lighted
  At one transcendent flame,
The wondrous Love, the perfect Love,
  Our Father's sweetest name;
For His Name and very Essence
  And His Will are all the same!

Conversely, in proportion as we see this splendour of His will,
we shall more readily or more fully surrender our own. Not until
we have presented our bodies a living sacrifice can we prove what
is that good, and perfect, and acceptable will of God. But in thus
proving it, this continual presentation will be more and more seen
to be our reasonable service, and becomes more and more a joyful
sacrifice of praise.

The connection in Romans xii. 1, 2, between our sacrifice which

He so graciously calls acceptable to Himself, and our finding out
that His will is acceptable to ourselves, is very striking. One reason for this connection may be that only love can really understand love, and love on both sides is at the bottom of the whole
transaction and its results. First, He loves us. Then the discovery
of this leads us to love Him. Then, because He loves us, He claims
us, and desires to have us wholly yielded to His will, so that the
operations of love in and for us may find no hindrance. Then,
because we love Him we recognise His claim and yield ourselves.
Then, being thus yielded, He draws us nearer to Him,[3] and admits
us, so to speak, into closer intimacy, so that we gain nearer and
truer views of His perfections. Then the unity of these perfections
becomes clearer to us. Now we not only see His justice and mercy
flowing in an undivided stream from the cross of Christ, but we
see that they never were divided, though the strange distortions
of the dark, false glass of sin made them appear so, but that both
are but emanations of God's holy love. Then having known and
believed this holy love, we see further that His will is not a sepa-
rate thing, but only love (and therefore all His attributes) in action; love being the primary essence of His being, and all the other
attributes manifestations and combinations of that ineffable essence, for God is Love. Then this will of God which has seemed in
old far-off days a stern and fateful power, is seen to be only love
energized; love saying, 'I will.' And when once we really grasp this
(hardly so much by faith as by love itself), the will of God cannot be
otherwise than acceptable, for it is no longer a question of trusting
that somehow or other there is a hidden element of love in it, but
of understanding that it is love; no more to be dissociated from it
than the power of the sun's rays can be dissociated from their light
and warmth. And love recognized must surely be love accepted
and reciprocated. So, as the fancied sternness of God's will is lost
in His love, the stubbornness of our will becomes melted in that
love, and lost in our acceptance of it.

'Take Thine own way with me, dear Lord,
  Thou canst not otherwise than bless;
I launch me forth upon a sea
  Of boundless love and tenderness.

'I could not choose a larger bliss
  Than to be wholly Thine; and mine
A will whose highest joy is this,
  To ceaselessly unclasp in Thine.

'I will not fear Thee, O my God!
  The days to come can only bring
Their perfect sequences of love,
  Thy larger, deeper comforting.

'Within the shadow of this love,
  Loss doth transmute itself to gain;
Faith veils earth's sorrows in its light,
  And straightway lives above her pain.

'We are not losers thus; we share
  The perfect gladness of the Son,
Not conquered—for, behold, we reign;
  Conquered and Conqueror are one.

'Thy wonderful grand will, my God!
  Triumphantly I make it mine;
And faith shall breathe her glad "Amen"
  To every dear command of Thine.

'Beneath the splendour of Thy choice,
  Thy perfect choice for me, I rest;
Outside it now I dare not live,
  Within it I must needs be blest.

'Meanwhile my spirit anchors calm
  In grander regions still than this;
The fair, far-shining latitudes
  Of that yet unexplorèd bliss.

'Then may Thy perfect, glorious will
  Be evermore fulfilled in me,
And make my life an answ'ring chord
  Of glad, responsive harmony.

'Oh! it is life indeed to live
  Within this kingdom strangely sweet,
And yet we fear to enter in,
  And linger with unwilling feet.

'We fear this wondrous rule of Thine,
  Because we have not reached Thy heart;
Not venturing our all on Thee,
  We may not know how good Thou art.'
    ~Jean Sophia Pigott.

[3] 'Now ye have consecrated yourselves unto the Lord, come near' (2 Chron. xxix. 31).

Chapter X
Our hearts kept for Jesus

'Keep my heart; it is Thine own;
It is now Thy royal throne.'

'It is a good thing that the heart be established with grace,' and yet some of us go on as if it were not a good thing even to hope for it to be so.

We should be ashamed to say that we had behaved treacherously to a friend; that we had played him false again and again; that we had said scores of times what we did not really mean; that we had professed and promised what, all the while, we had no sort of purpose of performing. We should be ready to go off by next ship to New Zealand rather than calmly own to all this, or rather than ever face our friends again after we had owned it. And yet we are not ashamed (some of us) to say that we are always dealing treacherously with our Lord; nay, more, we own it with an inexplicable complacency, as if there were a kind of virtue in saying how fickle and faithless and desperately wicked our hearts are; and we actually plume ourselves on the easy confession, which we think proves our humility, and which does not lower us in the eyes of others, nor in our own eyes, half so much as if we had to say, 'I have told a story,' or, 'I have broken my promise.' Nay, more, we have not the slightest hope, and therefore not the smallest intention of aiming at an utterly different state of things. Well for us if we do not go a step farther, and call those by hard and false names who do seek to have an established heart, and who believe that as the Lord meant what He said when He promised, 'No good thing will He withhold from them that walk uprightly,' so He will not withhold this good thing.

Prayer must be based upon promise, but, thank God, His promises are always broader than our prayers. No fear of building inverted pyramids here, for Jesus Christ is the foundation, and this and all the other 'promises of God in Him are yea, and in Him amen, unto the glory of God by us.' So it shall be unto His glory to fulfil this one to us, and to answer our prayer for a 'kept' or 'established' heart. And its fulfilment shall work out His glory, not in spite of us, but 'by us.'

We find both the means and the result of the keeping in the 112th Psalm: 'His heart is fixed.' Whose heart? An angel? A saint in glory? No! Simply the heart of the man that feareth the Lord, and delighteth greatly in His commandments. Therefore yours and mine, as God would have them be; just the normal idea of a God-fearing heart, nothing extremely and hopelessly beyond attainment.

'Fixed.' How does that tally with the deceitfulness and waywardness and fickleness about which we really talk as if we were rather proud of them than utterly ashamed of them?

Does our heavenly Bridegroom expect nothing more of us? Does His mighty, all-constraining love intend to do no more for us than to leave us in this deplorable state, when He is undoubtedly able to heal the desperately wicked heart (compare verses 9 and 14 of Jeremiah xvii.), to rule the wayward one with His peace, and to establish the fickle one with His grace? Are we not 'without excuse'?

'Fixed, trusting in the Lord.' Here is the means of the fixing— trust. He works the trust in us by sending the Holy Spirit to reveal God in Christ to us as absolutely, infinitely worthy of our trust. When we 'see Jesus' by Spirit-wrought faith, we cannot but trust Him; we distrust our hearts more truly than ever before, but we trust our Lord entirely, because we trust Him only. For, entrusting our trust to Him, we know that He is able to keep that which we commit (i. e. entrust) to Him. It is His own way of winning and fixing our hearts for Himself. Is it not a beautiful one? Thus 'his heart is established.' But we have not quite faith enough to believe that. So what is the very first doubting, and therefore sad thought that crops up? 'Yes, but I am afraid it will not remain fixed.'

That is your thought. Now see what is God's thought about the case. 'His heart is established, he shall not be afraid.'

Is not that enough? What is, if such plain and yet divine words are not? Well, the Gracious One bears with us, and gives line upon line to His poor little children. And so He says, 'The peace of God, which passeth all understanding, shall keep your hearts and minds, through Christ Jesus.' And again, 'Thy thoughts shall be established.' And again, 'Thou wilt keep him in perfect peace, whose mind is stayed on Thee, because he trusteth in Thee.'

And to prove to us that these promises can be realized in present experience, He sends down to us through nearly 3000 years the words of the man who prayed, 'Create in me a clean heart, O God,' and lets us hear twice over the new song put by the same

Holy Spirit into his mouth: 'My heart is fixed, O God, my heart is fixed' (Ps. lvii. 7, cviii. 1).

The heart that is established in Christ is also established for Christ. It becomes His royal throne, no longer occupied by His foe, no longer tottering and unstable. And then we see the beauty and preciousness of the promise, 'He shall be a Priest upon His throne.' Not only reigning, but atoning. Not only ruling, but cleansing. Thus the throne is established 'in mercy,' but 'by righteousness.'

I think we lose ground sometimes by parleying with the tempter. We have no business to parley with an usurper. The throne is no longer his when we have surrendered it to our Lord Jesus. And why should we allow him to argue with us for one instant, as if it were still an open question? Don't listen; simply tell him that Jesus Christ is on the long-disputed throne, and no more about it, but turn at once to your King and claim the glorious protection of His sovereignty over you. It is a splendid reality, and you will find it so. He will not abdicate and leave you kingless and defenceless. For verily, 'The Lord is our King; He will save us' (Isa. xxxiii. 22).

Our hearts are naturally—		God can make them—	
Evil,	Heb. iii. 12.	Clean,	Ps. li. 10.
Desperately wicked,		Jer. xvii. 9.	Good, Luke viii. 15.
Weak,	Ezek. xvi. 30.	Fixed,	Ps. cxii. 7.
Deceitful,	Jer. xvii. 9.	Faithful,	Neh. ix. 8.
Deceived,	Isa. xliv. 20.	Understanding,	1 Kings iii. 9.
Double,	Ps. xii. 2.	Honest,	Luke viii. 15.
Impenitent,	Rom. ii. 5.	Contrite,	Ps. li. 17.
Rebellious,	Jer. v. 23.	True,	Heb. x. 22.
Hard,	Ezek. iii. 7.	Soft,	Job xxiii. 16.
Stony,	Ezek. xi. 19.	New,	Ezek. xviii. 31.
Froward,	Prov. xvii. 20.	Sound,	Ps. cxix. 80.
Despiteful,	Ezek. xxv. 15.	Glad,	Ps. xvi. 9.
Stout,	Isa. x. 12.	Established,	Ps. cxii. 8.
Haughty,	Prov. xviii. 12.	Tender,	Ephes. iv. 32.
Proud,	Prov. xxi. 4.	Pure,	Matt. v. 8.
Perverse,	Prov. xii. 8.	Perfect,	1 Chron. xxix. 9.
Foolish,	Rom. i. 21.	Wise,	Prov. xi. 29.

Chapter XI
Our love kept for Jesus

'Keep my love; my Lord, I pour
At Thy feet its treasure-store.'

Not as a mere echo from the morning-gilded shore of Tiberias, but as an ever new, ever sounding note of divinest power, come the familiar words to each of us, 'Lovest thou Me?' He says it who has loved us with an everlasting love. He says it who has died for us. He says it who has washed us from our sins in His own blood. He says it who has waited for our love, waited patiently all through our coldness.

And if by His grace we have said, 'Take my love,' which of us has not felt that part of His very answer has been to make us see how little there was to take, and how little of that little has been kept for Him? And yet we do love Him! He knows that! The very mourning and longing to love Him more proves it. But we want more than that, and so does our Lord.

He has created us to love. We have a sealed treasure of love, which either remains sealed, and then gradually dries up and wastes away, or is unsealed and poured out, and yet is the fuller and not the emptier for the outpouring. The more love we give, the more we have to give. So far it is only natural. But when the Holy Spirit reveals the love of Christ, and sheds abroad the love of God in our hearts, this natural love is penetrated with a new principle as it discovers a new Object. Everything that it beholds in that Object gives it new depth and new colours. As it sees the holiness, the beauty, and the glory, it takes the deep hues of conscious sinfulness, unworthiness, and nothingness. As it sees even a glimpse of the love that passeth knowledge, it takes the glow of wonder and gratitude. And when it sees that love drawing close to its deepest need with blood-purchased pardon, it is intensified and stirred, and there is no more time for weighing and measuring; we must pour it out, all there is of it, with our tears, at the feet that were pierced for love of us.

And what then? Has the flow grown gradually slower and shallower? Has our Lord reason to say, 'My brethren have dealt deceitfully as a brook, and as a stream of brooks they pass away'? It is humiliating to have found that we could not keep on loving Him, as we loved in that remembered hour when 'Thy time was the time of love.' We have proved that we were not able. Let this be only the stepping-stone to proving that He is able!

There will have been a cause, as we shall see if we seek it honestly. It was not that we really poured out all our treasure, and so it naturally came to an end. We let it be secretly diverted into other channels. We began keeping back a little part of the price for something else. We looked away from, instead of looking away unto Jesus. We did not entrust Him with our love, and ask Him to keep it for Himself.

And what has He to say to us? Ah, He upbraideth not. Listen! 'Thus saith the Lord, I remember thee, the kindness of thy youth, the love of thine espousals.' Can any words be more tender, more touching, to you, to me? Forgetting all the sin, all the backsliding, all the coldness, casting all that into the unreturning depths of the sea, He says He remembers that hour when we first said, 'Take my love.' He remembers it now, at this minute. He has written it for ever on His infinite memory, where the past is as the present.

His own love is unchangeable, so it could never be His wish or will that we should thus drift away from Him. Oh, 'Come and let us return unto the Lord!' But is there any hope that, thus returning, our flickering love may be kept from again failing? Hear what He says: 'And I will betroth thee unto Me for ever' And again: 'Thou shalt abide for Me many days; so will I also be for thee.' Shall we trust His word or not? Is it worthy of our acceptation or not? Oh, rest on this word of the King, and let Him from this day have the keeping of your love, and He will keep it!

The love of Christ is not an absorbing, but a radiating love. The more we love Him, the more we shall most certainly love others. Some have not much natural power of loving, but the love of Christ will strengthen it. Some have had the springs of love dried up by some terrible earthquake. They will find 'fresh springs' in Jesus, and the gentle flow will be purer and deeper than the old torrent could ever be. Some have been satisfied that it should rush in a narrow channel, but He will cause it to overflow into many another, and widen its course of blessing. Some have spent it all on their God-given dear ones. Now He is come whose right it is; and yet in the fullest resumption of that right, He is so gracious that He puts back an even larger measure of the old love into our hand, sanctified with His own love, and energized with His blessing, and

strengthened with His new commandment, 'That ye love one another, as I have loved you.'

In that always very interesting part, called a 'Corner for Difficulties,' of that always very interesting magazine, Woman's Work, the
question has been discussed, 'When does love become idolatry? Is
it the experience of Christians that the coming in of a new object
of affection interferes with entire consecration to God?' I should
like to quote the many excellent answers in full, but must only
refer my readers to the number for March 1879. One replies: 'It
seems to me that He who is love would not give us an object for our
love unless He saw that our hearts needed expansion; and if the
love is consecrated, and the friendship takes its stand in Christ,
there is no need for the fear that it will become idolatry. Let the
love on both sides be given to God to keep, and however much it
may grow, the source from which it springs must yet be greater.'
Perhaps I may be pardoned for giving, at the same writer's suggestion, a quotation from Under the Surface on this subject. Eleanor
says to Beatrice:—

'I tremble when I think
How much I love him; but I turn away
From thinking of it, just to love him more;—
Indeed, I fear, too much.'

'Dear Eleanor,
Do you love him as much as Christ loves us?
Let your lips answer me.'
'Why ask me, dear?
Our hearts are finite, Christ is infinite.'
'Then, till you reach the standard of that love,
Let neither fears nor well-meant warning voice
Distress you with "too much." For He hath said
How much—and who shall dare to change His measure?
"That ye should love as I have loved you."
O sweet command, that goes so far beyond
The mightiest impulse of the tenderest heart!
A bare permission had been much; but He
Who knows our yearnings and our fearfulness,
Chose graciously to bid us do the thing
That makes our earthly happiness,
A limit that we need not fear to pass,
Because we cannot. Oh, the breadth and length,
And depth and height of love that passeth knowledge!

Yet Jesus said, "As I have loved you."'
 'O Beatrice, I long to feel the sunshine
That this should bring; but there are other words
Which fall in chill eclipse. 'Tis written, "Keep
Yourselves from idols." How shall I obey?'
 'Oh, not by loving less, but loving more.
It is not that we love our precious ones
Too much, but God too little. As the lamp
A miner bears upon his shadowed brow
Is only dazzling in the grimy dark,
And has no glare against the summer sky,
So, set the tiny torch of our best love
In the great sunshine of the love of God,
And, though full fed and fanned, it casts no shade
And dazzles not, o'erflowed with mightier light.'

There is no love so deep and wide as that which is kept for Jesus. It flows both fuller and farther when it flows only through Him. Then, too, it will be a power for Him. It will always be unconsciously working for Him. In drawing others to ourselves by it, we shall be necessarily drawing them nearer to the fountain of our love, never drawing them away from it. It is the great magnet of His love which alone can draw any heart to Him; but when our own are thoroughly yielded to its mighty influence, they will be so magnetized that He will condescend to use them in this way.

Is it not wonderful to think that the Lord Jesus will not only accept and keep, but actually use our love?

'Of Thine own have we given Thee,' for 'we love Him because He first loved us.'

Set apart to love Him,
 And His love to know;
Not to waste affection
 On a passing show;
Called to give Him life and heart,
 Called to pour the hidden treasure,
 That none other claims to measure,
Into His belovèd hand! thrice blessèd 'set apart'!

Chapter XII
Our Selves kept for Jesus

'Keep my self, that I may be
Ever, only, all for Thee.'

'For Thee!' That is the beginning and the end of the whole matter of consecration.

There was a prelude to its 'endless song,'—a prelude whose theme is woven into every following harmony in the new anthem of consecrated life: 'The Son of God, who loved me, and gave Himself for me.' Out of the realized 'for me,' grows the practical 'for Thee!' If the former is a living root, the latter will be its living fruit.

'For Thee!' This makes the difference between forced or formal, and therefore unreasonable service, and the 'reasonable service' which is the beginning of the perfect service where they see His face. This makes the difference between slave work and free work. For Thee, my Redeemer; for Thee who hast spoken to my heart; for Thee, who hast done for me—what? Let us each pause, and fill up that blank with the great things the Lord hath done for us. For Thee, who art to me—what? Fill that up too, before Him! For Thee, my Saviour Jesus, my Lord and my God!

And what is to be for Him? My self. We talk sometimes as if, whatever else could be subdued unto Him, self could never be. Did St. Paul forget to mention this important exception to the 'all things' in Phil. iii. 21? David said: 'Bless the Lord, O my soul, and all that is within me, bless His Holy Name.' Did he, too, unaccountably forget to mention that he only meant all that was within him, except self? If not, then self must be among the 'all things' which the Lord Jesus Christ is able to subdue unto Himself, and which are to 'bless His Holy Name.' It is Self which, once His most treacherous foe, is now, by full and glad surrender, His own soldier—coming over from the rebel camp into the royal army. It is not some one else, some temporarily possessing spirit, which says within us, 'Lord, Thou knowest that I love Thee,' but our true and very self, only changed and renewed by the power of the Holy Ghost. And when we do that we would not, we know that 'it is no more I that do it, but sin that dwelleth in me.' Our true self is the new self, taken and won by the love of God, and kept by the power of God.

Yes, 'kept!' There is the promise on which we ground our prayer; or, rather, one of the promises. For, search and look for your own strengthening and comfort, and you will find it repeated in every part of the Bible, from 'I am with thee, and will keep thee,' in Genesis, to 'I also will keep thee from the hour of temptation,' in Revelation.

And kept for Him! Why should it be thought a thing incredible with you, when it is only the fulfilling of His own eternal purpose in creating us? 'This people have I formed for Myself.' Not ultimately only, but presently and continually; for He says, 'Thou shalt abide for Me;' and, 'He that remaineth, even he shall be for our God.' Are you one of His people by faith in Jesus Christ? Then see what you are to Him. You, personally and individually, are part of the Lord's portion (Deut. xxxii. 9) and of His inheritance (1 Kings viii. 53, and Eph. i. 18). His portion and inheritance would not be complete without you; you are His peculiar treasure (Ex. xix. 5); 'a special people' (how warm, and loving, and natural that expression is!) 'unto Himself' (Deut. vii. 6). Would you call it 'keeping,' if you had a 'special' treasure, a darling little child, for instance, and let it run wild into all sorts of dangers all day long, sometimes at your side, and sometimes out in the street, with only the intention of fetching it safe home at night? If ye then, being evil, would know better, and do better, than that, how much more shall our Lord's keeping be true, and tender, and continual, and effectual, when He declares us to be His peculiar treasure, purchased (See 1 Pet. ii. 9, margin) for Himself at such unknown cost!

> He will keep what thus He sought,
> Safely guard the dearly bought;
> Cherish that which He did choose,
> Always love and never lose.

I know what some of us are thinking. 'Yes; I see it all plainly enough in theory, but in practice I find I am not kept. Self goes over to the other camp again and again. If is not all for Jesus, though I have asked and wished for it to be so.' Dear friends, the 'all' must be sealed with 'only.' Are you willing to be 'only' for Jesus? You have not given 'all' to Jesus while you are not quite ready to be 'only' for Him. And it is no use to talk about 'ever' while we have not settled the 'only' and the 'all.' You cannot be 'for Him,' in the full and blessed sense, while you are partly 'for' anything or any one else. For 'the Lord hath set apart him that is godly for Himself.' You see, the 'for Himself' hinges upon the 'set apart.' There is no consecration without separation. If you are mourning over want of realized consecration, will you look humbly and sincerely into this point? 'A garden enclosed is my sister, my spouse,' saith the Heavenly Bridegroom.

> Set apart for Jesus!
>   Is not this enough,
> Though the desert prospect
>   Open wild and rough?
> Set apart for His delight,
>   Chosen for His holy pleasure,
>   Sealed to be His special treasure!
> Could we choose a nobler joy?—and would we, if we might?[4]

But yielding, by His grace, to this blessed setting apart for Himself, 'The Lord shall establish thee an holy people unto Himself, as He hath sworn unto thee.' Can there be a stronger promise? Just obey and trust His word now, and yield yourselves now unto God, 'that He may establish thee to-day for a people unto Himself.' Commit the keeping of your souls to Him in well-doing, as unto a faithful Creator, being persuaded that He is able to keep that which you commit to Him.

> Now, Lord, I give myself to Thee,
>   I would be wholly Thine,
> As Thou hast given Thyself to me,
>   And Thou art wholly mine;
> O take me, seal me for Thine own,
> Thine altogether, Thine alone.

Here comes in once more that immeasurably important subject of our influence. For it is not what we say or do, so much as what we are, that influences others. We have heard this, and very likely repeated it again and again, but have we seen it to be inevitably linked with the great question of this chapter? I do not know anything which, thoughtfully considered, makes us realize more vividly the need and the importance of our whole selves being kept for Jesus. Any part not wholly committed, and not wholly kept, must hinder and neutralize the real influence for Him of all the rest. If we ourselves are kept all for Jesus, then our influence will be all kept for Him too. If not, then, however much we may wish and talk and try, we cannot throw our full weight into the right scale. And just in so far as it is not in the one scale, it must be in the other; weighing against the little which we have tried to put in the right one, and making the short weight still shorter.

So large a proportion of it is entirely involuntary, while yet the responsibility of it is so enormous, that our helplessness comes out in exceptionally strong relief, while our past debt in this matter is simply incalculable. Are we feeling this a little? getting just a glimpse, down the misty defiles of memory, of the neutral influence, the wasted influence, the mistaken influence, the actually wrong influence which has marked the ineffaceable although untraceable course? And all the while we owed Him all that influence! It ought to have been all for Him! We have nothing to say. But what has our Lord to say? 'I forgave thee all that debt!'

Then, after that forgiveness which must come first, there comes a thought of great comfort in our freshly felt helplessness, rising out of the very thing that makes us realize this helplessness. Just because our influence is to such a great extent involuntary and unconscious, we may rest assured that if we ourselves are truly kept for Jesus, this will be, as a quite natural result, kept for Him also. It cannot be otherwise, for as is the fountain, so will be the flow; as the spring, so the action; as the impulse, so the communicated motion. Thus there may be, and in simple trust there will be, a quiet rest about it, a relief from all sense of strain and effort, a fulfilling of the words, 'For he that is entered into his rest, he also hath ceased from his own works, as God did from His.' It will not be a matter of trying to have good influence, but just of having it, as naturally and constantly as the magnetized bar.

Another encouraging thought should follow. Of ourselves we may have but little weight, no particular talents or position or anything else to put into the scale; but let us remember that again and again God has shown that the influence of a very average life, when once really consecrated to Him, may outweigh that of almost any number of merely professing Christians. Such lives are like Gideon's three hundred, carrying not even the ordinary weapons of war, but only trumpets and lamps and empty pitchers, by whom the Lord wrought great deliverance, while He did not use the others at all. For He hath chosen the weak things of the world to confound the things which are mighty.

Should not all this be additional motive for desiring that our whole selves should be taken and kept?

I know that whatsoever God doeth, it shall be for ever. Therefore we may rejoicingly say 'ever' as well as 'only' and 'all for Thee!' For the Lord is our Keeper, and He is the Almighty and the Everlasting God, with whom is no variableness, neither shadow of turning. He will never change His mind about keeping us, and no man is able to pluck us out of His hand. Neither will Christ let us pluck ourselves out of His hand, for He says, 'Thou shalt abide for Me many days.' And He that keepeth us will not slumber. Once having undertaken His vineyard, He will keep it night and day, till all the days and nights are over, and we know the full meaning of the salvation ready to be revealed in the last time, unto which we are kept by His power.

And then, for ever for Him! passing from the gracious keeping by faith for this little while, to the glorious keeping in His presence for all eternity! For ever fulfilling the object for which He formed us and chose us, we showing forth His praise, and He showing the exceeding riches of His grace in His kindness towards us in the ages to come! He for us, and we for Him for ever! Oh, how little we can grasp this! Yet this is the fruition of being 'kept for Jesus!'

Set apart for ever
  For Himself alone!
Now we see our calling
  Gloriously shown.
Owning, with no secret dread,
  This our holy separation,
  Now the crown of consecration[5]
Of the Lord our God shall rest upon our willing head.

---

[4] Loyal Responses, p. 11.
[5] Num. vi. 7.

Chapter XIII
Christ for Us

'So will I also be for Thee.'—Hos. iii. 3.

The typical promise, 'Thou shalt abide for Me many days,' is indeed a marvel of love. For it is given to the most undeserving, described under the strongest possible figure of utter worthlessness and treacherousness,—the woman beloved, yet an adulteress.

The depth of the abyss shows the length of the line that has fathomed it, yet only the length of the line reveals the real depth of the abyss. The sin shows the love, and the love reveals the sin. The Bible has few words more touching, though seldom quoted, than those just preceding this wonderful promise: 'The love of the Lord toward the children of Israel, who look to other gods, and love flagons of wine.' Put that into the personal application which no doubt underlies it, and say, 'The love of the Lord toward me, who have looked away from Him, with wandering, faithless eyes, to other helps and hopes, and have loved earthly joys and sought earthly gratifications,—the love of the Lord toward even me!' And then hear Him saying in the next verse, 'So I bought her to Me;' stooping to do that in His unspeakable condescension of love, not with the typical silver and barley, but with the precious blood of Christ. Then, having thus loved us, and rescued us, and bought us with a price indeed, He says, still under the same figure, 'Thou shalt abide for Me many days.'

This is both a command and a pledge. But the very pledge implies our past unfaithfulness, and the proved need of even our own part being undertaken by the ever patient Lord. He Himself has to guarantee our faithfulness, because there is no other hope of our continuing faithful. Well may such love win our full and glad surrender, and such a promise win our happy and confident trust!

But He says more. He says, 'So will I also be for thee!' And this seems an even greater marvel of love, as we observe how He meets every detail of our consecration with this wonderful word.[6]

1. His Life 'for thee!' 'The Good Shepherd giveth His life for the sheep.' Oh, wonderful gift! not promised, but given; not to friends, but to enemies. Given without condition, without reserve, with-

out return. Himself unknown and unloved, His gift unsought and unasked, He gave His life for thee; a more than royal bounty—the greatest gift that Deity could devise. Oh, grandeur of love! 'I lay down My life for the sheep!' And we for whom He gave it have held back, and hesitated to give our lives, not even for Him (He has not asked us to do that), but to Him! But that is past, and He has tenderly pardoned the unloving, ungrateful reserve, and has graciously accepted the poor little fleeting breath and speck of dust which was all we had to offer. And now His precious death and His glorious life are all 'for thee.'

2. His Eternity 'for thee.' All we can ask Him to take are days and moments—the little span given us as it is given, and of this only the present in deed and the future in will. As for the past, in so far as we did not give it to Him, it is too late; we can never give it now! But His past was given to us, though ours was not given to Him. Oh, what a tremendous debt does this show us!

Away back in the dim depths of past eternity, 'or ever the earth and the world were made,' His divine existence in the bosom of His Father was all 'for thee,' purposing and planning 'for thee,' receiving and holding the promise of eternal life 'for thee.'

Then the thirty-three years among sinners on this sinful earth: do we think enough of the slowly-wearing days and nights, the heavy-footed hours, the never-hastening minutes, that went to make up those thirty-three years of trial and humiliation? We all know how slowly time passes when suffering and sorrow are near, and there is no reason to suppose that our Master was exempted from this part of our infirmities.

Then His present is 'for thee.' Even now He 'liveth to make intercession;' even now He 'thinketh upon me;' even now He 'knoweth,' He 'careth,' He 'loveth.'

Then, only to think that His whole eternity will be 'for thee!' Millions of ages of unfoldings of all His love, and of ever new declarings of His Father's name to His brethren. Think of it! and can we ever hesitate to give all our poor little hours to His service?

3. His Hands 'for thee.' Literal hands; literally pierced, when the whole weight of His quivering frame hung from their torn muscles and bared nerves; literally uplifted in parting blessing. Consecrated, priestly hands; 'filled' hands (Ex. xxviii. 41, xxix. 9, etc., margin)—filled once with His great offering, and now with gifts and blessings 'for thee.' Tender hands, touching and healing, lifting and leading with gentlest care. Strong hands, upholding and defending. Open hands, filling with good and satisfying desire (Ps.

civ. 28, and cxlv. 16). Faithful hands, restraining and sustaining. 'His left hand is under my head, and His right hand doth embrace me.'

4. His Feet 'for thee.' They were weary very often, they were wounded and bleeding once. They made clear footprints as He went about doing good, and as He went up to Jerusalem to suffer; and these 'blessed steps of His most holy life,' both as substitution and example, were 'for thee.' Our place of waiting and learning, of resting and loving, is at His feet. And still those 'blessed feet' are and shall be 'for thee,' until He comes again to receive us unto Himself, until and when the word is fulfilled, 'They shall walk with Me in white.'

5. His Voice 'for thee.' The 'Voice of my beloved that knocketh, saying, Open to me, my sister, my love;' the Voice that His sheep 'hear' and 'know,' and that calls out the fervent response, 'Master, say on!' This is not all. It was the literal voice of the Lord Jesus which uttered that one echoless cry of desolation on the Cross 'for thee,' and it will be His own literal voice which will say, 'Come, ye blessed!' to thee. And that same tender and 'glorious Voice' has literally sung and will sing 'for thee.' I think He consecrated song for us, and made it a sweet and sacred thing for ever, when He Himself 'sang an hymn,' the very last thing before He went forth to consecrate suffering for us. That was not His last song. 'The Lord thy God ... will joy over thee with singing.' And the time is coming when He will not only sing 'for thee' or 'over thee,' but with thee. He says He will! 'In the midst of the church will I sing praise unto Thee.' Now what a magnificent glimpse of joy this is! 'Jesus Himself leading the praises of His brethren,[7] and we ourselves singing not merely in such a chorus, but with such a leader! If 'singing for Jesus' is such delight here, what will this 'singing with Jesus' be? Surely song may well be a holy thing to us henceforth.

6. His Lips 'for thee.' Perhaps there is no part of our consecration which it is so difficult practically to realize, and in which it is, therefore, so needful to recollect?—'I also for thee.' It is often helpful to read straight through one or more of the Gospels with a special thought on our mind, and see how much bears upon it. When we read one through with this thought—'His lips for me!'— wondering, verse by verse, at the grace which was poured into them, and the gracious words which fell from them, wondering more and more at the cumulative force and infinite wealth of tenderness and power and wisdom and love flowing from them, we cannot but desire that our lips and all the fruit of them should be

wholly for Him. 'For thee' they were opened in blessing; 'for thee' they were closed when He was led as a lamb to the slaughter. And whether teaching, warning, counsel, comfort, or encourage-ment, commandments in whose keeping there is a great reward, or promises which exceed all we ask or think—all the precious fruit of His lips is 'for thee,' really and truly meant 'for thee.'

7. His Wealth 'for thee.' 'Though He was rich, yet for our sakes He became poor, that ye through His poverty might be made rich.' Yes, 'through His poverty' the unsearchable riches of Christ are 'for thee.' Seven-fold riches are mentioned; and these are no un-minted treasure or sealed reserve, but all ready coined for our use, and stamped with His own image and superscription, and poured freely into the hand of faith. The mere list is wonderful. 'Riches of goodness,' 'riches of forbearance and long-suffering,' 'riches both of wisdom and knowledge,' 'riches of mercy,' 'exceeding riches of grace,' and 'riches of glory.' And His own Word says, 'All are yours!' Glance on in faith, and think of eternity flowing on and on beyond the mightiest sweep of imagination, and realize that all 'His riches in glory' and 'the riches of His glory' are and shall be 'for thee!' In view of this, shall we care to reserve anything that rust doth cor-rupt for ourselves?

8. His 'treasures of wisdom and knowledge' 'for thee.' First, used for our behalf and benefit. Why did He expend such immeasur-able might of mind upon a world which is to be burnt up, but that He would fit it perfectly to be, not the home, but the school of His children? The infinity of His skill is such that the most powerful intellects find a lifetime too short to penetrate a little way into a few secrets of some one small department of His working. If we turn to Providence, it is quite enough to take only one's own life, and look at it microscopically and telescopically, and marvel at the treasures of wisdom lavished upon its details, ordering and shaping and fitting the tiny confused bits into the true mosaic which He means it to be. Many a little thing in our lives reveals the same Mind which, according to a well-known and very beautiful illustration, adjusted a perfect proportion in the delicate hinges of the snowdrop and the droop of its bell, with the mass of the globe and the force of gravitation. How kind we think it if a very talented friend spends a little of his thought and power of mind in teach-ing us or planning for us! Have we been grateful for the infinite thought and wisdom which our Lord has expended upon us and our creation, preservation, and redemption?

Secondly, to be shared with us. He says, 'All that I have is thine.'

He holds nothing back, reserves nothing from His dear children, and what we cannot receive now He is keeping for us. He gives us 'hidden riches of secret places' now, but by and by He will give us more, and the glorified intellect will be filled continually out of His treasures of wisdom and knowledge. But the sanctified intellect will be, must be, used for Him, and only for Him, now!

9. His Will 'for thee.' Think first of the infinite might of that will; the first great law and the first great force of the universe, from which alone every other law and every other force has sprung, and to which all are subordinate. 'He worketh all things after the counsel of His own will.' 'He doeth according to His will in the army of heaven, and among the inhabitants of the earth.' Then think of the infinite mysteries of that will. For ages and generations the hosts of heaven have wonderingly watched its vouchsafed unveilings and its sublime developments, and still they are waiting, watching, and wondering.

Creation and Providence are but the whisper of its power, but Redemption is its music, and praise is the echo which shall yet fill His temple. The whisper and the music, yes, and 'the thunder of His power,' are all 'for thee.' For what is 'the good pleasure of His will'? (Eph. i. 5.) Oh, what a grand list of blessings purposed, provided, purchased, and possessed, all flowing to us out of it! And nothing but blessings, nothing but privileges, which we never should have imagined, and which, even when revealed, we are 'slow of heart to believe;' nothing but what should even now fill us 'with joy unspeakable and full of glory!'

Think of this will as always and altogether on our side—always working for us, and in us, and with us, if we will only let it; think of it as always and only synonymous with infinitely wise and almighty love; think of it as undertaking all for us, from the great work of our eternal salvation down to the momentary details of guidance and supply, and do we not feel utter shame and self-abhorrence at ever having hesitated for an instant to give up our tiny, feeble, blind will, to be—not crushed, not even bent, but blent with His glorious and perfect Will?

10. His Heart 'for thee.' 'Behold ... He is mighty ... in heart,' said Job (Job xxxvi. 5, margin). And this mighty and tender heart is 'for thee!' If He had only stretched forth His hand to save us from bare destruction, and said, 'My hand for thee!' how could we have praised Him enough? But what shall we say of the unspeakably marvellous condescension which says, 'Thou hast ravished (margin, taken away) my heart, my sister, my spouse!' The very fountain

of His divine life, and light, and love, the very centre of His being, is given to His beloved ones, who are not only 'set as a seal upon His heart,' but taken into His heart, so that our life is hid there, and we dwell there in the very centre of all safety, and power, and love, and glory. What will be the revelation of 'that day,' when the Lord Jesus promises, 'Ye shall know that I am in My Father, and ye in Me'? For He implies that we do not yet know it, and that our present knowledge of this dwelling in Him is not knowledge at all compared with what He is going to show us about it.

Now shall we, can we, reserve any corner of our hearts from Him?

11. His Love 'for thee.' Not a passive, possible love, but out-flowing, yes, outpouring of the real, glowing, personal love of His mighty and tender heart. Love not as an attribute, a quality, a latent force, but an acting, moving, reaching, touching, and grasp-ing power. Love, not a cold, beautiful, far-off star, but a sunshine that comes and enfolds us, making us warm and glad, and strong and bright and fruitful.

His love! What manner of love is it? What should be quoted to prove or describe it? First the whole Bible with its mysteries and marvels of redemption, then the whole book of Providence and the whole volume of creation. Then add to these the unknown records of eternity past and the unknown glories of eternity to come, and then let the immeasurable quotation be sung by 'angels and arch-angels, and all the company of heaven,' with all the harps of God, and still that love will be untold, still it will be 'the love of Christ that passeth knowledge.'

But it is 'for thee!'

12. Himself 'for thee.' 'Christ also hath loved us, and given Him-self for us.' 'The Son of God ... loved me, and gave Himself for me.' Yes, Himself! What is the Bride's true and central treasure? What calls forth the deepest, brightest, sweetest thrill of love and praise? Not the Bridegroom's priceless gifts, not the robe of His resplendent righteousness, not the dowry of unsearchable riches, not the magnificence of the palace home to which He is bringing her, not the glory which she shall share with Him, but Himself! Jesus Christ, 'who His own self bare our sins in His own body on the tree;' 'this same Jesus,' 'whom having not seen, ye love;' the Son of God, and the Man of Sorrows; my Saviour, my Friend, my Master, my King, my Priest, my Lord and my God—He says, 'I also for thee!' What an 'I'! What power and sweetness we feel in it, so different from any human 'I,' for all His Godhead and all His man-

hood are concentrated in it, and all 'for thee!'

And not only 'all,' but 'ever' for thee. His unchangeableness is the seal upon every attribute; He will be 'this same Jesus' for ever. How can mortal mind estimate this enormous promise? How can mortal heart conceive what is enfolded in these words, 'I also for thee'?

One glimpse of its fulness and glory, and we feel that henceforth it must be, shall be, and by His grace will be our true-hearted, whole-hearted cry—

Take myself, and I will be
Ever, ONLY, ALL for Thee!

[6] The remainder of this chapter is printed in a little penny book, entitled, I also for Thee, by F. R. H., published by Caswell, Birmingham, and by Nisbet & Co.

[7] See A. Newton on the Epistle to the Hebrews, ch. ii. ver. 12.

SELECTIONS FROM
MISS HAVERGAL'S LATEST POEMS

An Interlude

That part is finished! I lay down my pen,
  And wonder if the thoughts will flow as fast
Through the more difficult defile. For the last
  Was easy, and the channel deeper then.
My Master, I will trust Thee for the rest;
Give me just what Thou wilt, and that will be my best!

How can I tell the varied, hidden need
  Of Thy dear children, all unknown to me,
Who at some future time may come and read
  What I have written! All are known to Thee.
As Thou hast helped me, help me to the end;
Give me Thy own sweet messages of love to send.

So now, I pray Thee, keep my hand in Thine;
  And guide it as Thou wilt. I do not ask
To understand the 'wherefore' of each line;
  Mine is the sweeter, easier, happier task,
  Just to look up to Thee for every word,
Rest in Thy love, and trust, and know that I am heard.

The Thoughts of God

They say there is a hollow, safe and still,
  A point of coolness and repose
Within the centre of a flame, where life might dwell
Unharmed and unconsumed, as in a luminous shell,
  Which the bright walls of fire enclose
In breachless splendour, barrier that no foes
Could pass at will.

There is a point of rest
  At the great centre of the cyclone's force,
A silence at its secret source;—
A little child might slumber undistressed,
  Without the ruffle of one fairy curl,
In that strange central calm amid the mighty whirl.

So, in the centre of these thoughts of God,
Cyclones of power, consuming glory-fire,—
 As we fall o'erawed
Upon our faces, and are lifted higher
By His great gentleness, and carried nigher
Than unredeemèd angels, till we stand
 Even in the hollow of His hand,
 Nay, more! we lean upon His breast—
There, there we find a point of perfect rest
 And glorious safety. There we see
 His thoughts to usward, thoughts of peace
That stoop in tenderest love; that still increase
With increase of our need; that never change,
That never fail, or falter, or forget
 O pity infinite!
 O royal mercy free!
 O gentle climax of the depth and height
Of God's most precious thoughts, most wonderful, most strange!
 'For I am poor and needy, yet
The Lord Himself, Jehovah, thinketh upon me!'

'Free to Serve.'

She chose His service. For the Lord of Love
Had chosen her, and paid the awful price
For her redemption; and had sought her out,
And set her free, and clothed her gloriously,
And put His royal ring upon her hand,
And crowns of loving-kindness on her head.
She chose it. Yet it seemed she could not yield
The fuller measure other lives could bring;
For He had given her a precious gift,
A treasure and a charge to prize and keep,
A tiny hand, a darling hand, that traced
On her heart's tablet words of golden love.
And there was not much room for other lines,
For time and thought were spent (and rightly spent,
For He had given the charge), and hours and days
Were concentrated on the one dear task.
But He had need of her. Not one new gem
But many for His crown;—not one fair sheaf,
But many, she should bring. And she should have

A richer, happier harvest-home at last.
Because more fruit, more glory and more praise
Her life should yield to Him. And so He came,
The Master came Himself, and gently took
The little hand in His, and gave it room
Among the angel-harpers. Jesus came
And laid His own hand on the quivering heart,
And made it very still, that He might write
Invisible words of power—'Free to serve!'
Then through the darkness and the chill He sent
A heat-ray of His love, developing
The mystic writing, till it glowed and shone
And lit up all her life with radiance new,—
The happy service of a yielded heart.
With comfort that He never ceased to give
(Because her need could never cease) she filled
The empty chalices of other lives,
And time and thought were thenceforth spent for Him
Who loved her with His everlasting love.
Let Him write what He will upon our hearts,

With His unerring pen. They are His own,
Hewn from the rock by His selecting grace,
Prepared for His own glory. Let Him write!
Be sure He will not cross out one sweet word
But to inscribe a sweeter,—but to grave
One that shall shine for ever to His praise,
And thus fulfil our deepest heart-desire.
The tearful eye at first may read the line,
'Bondage to grief!' But He shall wipe away
The tears, and clear the vision, till it read
In ever-brightening letters, 'Free to serve!'
For whom the Son makes free is free indeed.
Nor only by reclaiming His good gifts,
But by withholding, doth the Master write
These words upon the heart. Not always needs
Erasure of some blessèd line of love
For this more blest inscription. Where He finds
A tablet empty for the 'lines left out,'
That 'might have been' engraved with human love
And sweetest human cares, yet never bore
That poetry of life, His own dear hand

Writes 'Free to serve!' And these clear characters
Fill with fair colours all the unclaimed space,
Else grey and colourless.

  Then let it be
The motto of our lives until we stand
In the great freedom of Eternity,
Where we 'shall serve Him' while we see His face,
For ever and for ever 'Free to serve.'

Coming to the King.

2 Chronicles ix. 1-12.

I came from very far away to see
  The King of Salem; for I had been told
  Of glory and of wisdom manifold,
And condescension infinite and free.
How could I rest, when I had heard His fame,
In that dark lonely land of death from whence I came?

I came (but not like Sheba's queen), alone!
  No stately train, no costly gifts to bring;
  No friend at court, save One, that One the King!
I had requests to spread before His throne,
And I had questions none could solve for me,
Of import deep, and full of awful mystery.

I came and communed with that mighty King,
  And told Him all my heart; I cannot say,
  In mortal ear, what communings were they.
But wouldst thou know, go too, and meekly bring
All that is in thy heart, and thou shalt hear
His voice of love and power, His answers sweet and clear.

O happy end of every weary quest!
  He told me all I needed, graciously;—
  Enough for guidance, and for victory
O'er doubts and fears, enough for quiet rest;
And when some veiled response I could not read,
It was not hid from Him,—this was enough indeed.

His wisdom and His glories passed before
  My wondering eyes in gradual revelation;
  The house that He had built, its strong foundation,
Its living stones; and, brightening more and more,

Fair glimpses of that palace far away,
Where all His loyal ones shall dwell with Him for aye.

True the report that reached my far-off land
  Of all His wisdom and transcendent fame;
  Yet I believed not until I came,—
Bowed to the dust till raised by royal hand.
The half was never told by mortal word;
My King exceeded all the fame that I had heard!

Oh, happy are His servants! happy they
  Who stand continually before His face,
  Ready to do His will of wisest grace!
My King! is mine such blessedness to-day?
For I too hear Thy wisdom, line by line,
Thy ever brightening words in holy radiance shine.

Oh, blessèd be the Lord thy God, who set
  Our King upon His throne! Divine delight
  In the Beloved crowning Thee with might,
Honour, and majesty supreme; and yet
The strange and Godlike secret opening thus,—
The kingship of His Christ ordained through love to us!

What shall I render to my glorious King?
  I have but that which I receive from Thee;
  And what I give, Thou givest back to me,
Transmuted by Thy touch; each worthless thing
Changed to the preciousness of gem or gold,
And by Thy blessing multiplied a thousand fold.

All my desire Thou grantest, whatsoe'er
  I ask! Was ever mythic tale or dream
  So bold as this reality,—this stream
Of boundless blessings flowing full and free?
Yet more than I have thought or asked of Thee,
Out of Thy royal bounty still Thou givest me.

Now I will turn to my own land, and tell
  What I myself have seen and heard of Thee.
  And give Thine own sweet message, 'Come and see!'
And yet in heart and mind for ever dwell
With Thee, my King of Peace, in loyal rest,
Within the fair pavilion of Thy presence blest.

'Surely in what place my Lord the King shall be, whether in death
or life, even there also will thy servant be.'—2 Sam. xv. 21.

'Where I am, there shall also my servant be.'—John xii. 26.

The Two Paths.
Via Dolorosa and Via Giojosa.
[Suggested by a Picture.]

My Master, they have wronged Thee and Thy love!
They only told me I should find the path
A Via Dolorosa all the way!
Even Thy sweetest singers only sang
Of pressing onward through the same sharp thorns,
With bleeding footsteps, through the chill dark mist,
Following and struggling till they reach the light,
The rest, the sunshine of the far beyond.
The anthems of the pilgrimage were set
In most pathetic minors, exquisite,
Yet breathing sadness more than any praise;
Thy minstrels let the fitful breezes make
Æolian moans on their entrusted harps,
Until the listeners thought that this was all
The music Thou hadst given. And so the steps
That halted where the two ways met and crossed,
The broad and narrow, turned aside in fear,
Thinking the radiance of their youth must pass
In sombre shadows if they followed Thee;
Hearing afar such echoes of one strain,
The cross, the tribulation, and the toil,
The conflict, and the clinging in the dark.
What wonder that the dancing feet are stayed
From entering the only path of peace!
Master, forgive them! Tune their harps anew,
And put a new song in their mouths for Thee,
And make Thy chosen people joyful in Thy love.

Lord Jesus, Thou hast trodden once for all
The Via Dolorosa,—and for us!
No artist power or minstrel gift may tell
The cost to Thee of each unfaltering step,
When love that passeth knowledge led Thee on,
Faithful and true to God, and true to us.

And now, belovèd Lord, Thou callest us
To follow Thee, and we will take Thy word
About the path which Thou hast marked for us.
Narrow indeed it is! Who does not choose
The narrow track upon the mountain side,
With ever-widening view, and freshening air,
And honeyed heather, rather than the road,
With smoothest breadth of dust and loss of view,
Soiled blossoms not worth gathering, and the noise
Of wheels instead of silence of the hills,
Or music of the waterfalls? Oh, why
Should they misrepresent Thy words, and make
'Narrow' synonymous with 'very hard'?
 For Thou, Divinest Wisdom, Thou hast said
Thy ways are ways of pleasantness, and all
Thy paths are peace; and that the path of him
Who wears Thy perfect robe of righteousness
Is as the light that shineth more and more
Unto the perfect day. And Thou hast given
An olden promise, rarely quoted now,[8]
Because it is too bright for our weak faith:
'If they obey and serve Him, they shall spend
Days in prosperity, and they shall spend
Their years in pleasures.' All because Thy days
Were full of sorrow, and Thy lonely years
Were passed in grief's acquaintance—all for us!

Master, I set my seal that Thou art true,
Of Thy good promise not one thing hath failed!
And I would send a ringing challenge forth,
To all who know Thy name, to tell it out,
Thy faithfulness to every written word,
Thy loving-kindness crowning all the days,—
To say and sing with me: 'The Lord is good,
His mercy is for ever, and His truth
Is written on each page of all my life!'
Yes! there is tribulation, but Thy power
Can blend it with rejoicing. There are thorns,
But they have kept us in the narrow way,
The King's Highway of holiness and peace.
And there is chastening, but the Father's love
Flows through it; and would any trusting heart

Forego the chastening and forego the love?
And every step leads on to 'more and more,'
From strength to strength Thy pilgrims pass and sing
The praise of Him who leads them on and on,
From glory unto glory, even here!

[8] Job xxvi. 15.

Only for Jesus

Only for Jesus! Lord, keep it for ever
Sealed on the heart and engraved on the life!
Pulse of all gladness and nerve of endeavour,
Secret of rest, and the strength of our strife.

'Vessels of Mercy, Prepared unto Glory.'
(Rom. ix. 23.)

Vessels of mercy, prepared unto glory!
 This is your calling and this is your joy!
This, for the new year unfolding before ye,
 Tells out the terms of your blessed employ.

Vessels, it may be, all empty and broken,
 Marred in the Hand of inscrutable skill;
(Love can accept the mysterious token!)
 Marred but to make them more beautiful still.
 Jer. xviii. 4.

Vessels, it may be, not costly or golden;
 Vessels, it may be, of quantity small,
Yet by the Nail in the Sure Place upholden,
 Never to shiver and never to fall.
 Isa. xxii. 23, 24.

Vessels to honour, made sacred and holy,
 Meet for the use of the Master we love,
Ready for service, all simple and lowly,
 Ready, one day, for the temple above.
 2 Tim. ii. 21.

Yes, though the vessels be fragile and earthen,
 God hath commanded His glory to shine;
Treasure resplendent henceforth is our burthen,
 Excellent power, not ours but Divine.
 2 Cor. iv. 5, 6.

Chosen in Christ ere the dawn of Creation,
  Chosen for Him, to be filled with His grace,
Chosen to carry the streams of salvation
  Into each thirsty and desolate place.
    Acts ix. 15.

Take all Thy vessels, O glorious Finer,
  Purge all the dross, that each chalice may be
Pure in Thy pattern, completer, diviner,
  Filled with Thy glory and shining for Thee.
    Prov. xxv. 4.

The Turned Lesson

'I thought I knew it!' she said,
  'I thought I had learnt it quite!'
But the gentle Teacher shook her head,
  With a grave yet loving light
In the eyes that fell on the upturned face,
  As she gave the book
With the mark still set in the self-same place.

'I thought I knew it!' she said;
  And a heavy tear fell down,
As she turned away with bending head,
  Yet not for reproof or frown,
Not for the lesson to learn again,
  Or the play hour lost;—
It was something else that gave the pain.

She could not have put it in words,
  But her Teacher understood,
As God understands the chirp of the birds
  In the depth of an autumn wood.
And a quiet touch on the reddening cheek
  Was quite enough;
No need to question, no need to speak.

Then the gentle voice was heard,
  'Now I will try you again!'
And the lesson was mastered,—every word!
  Was it not worth the pain?
Was it not kinder the task to turn,
  Than to let it pass,
As a lost, lost leaf that she did not learn?

Is it not often so,
  That we only learn in part,
And the Master's testing-time may show
  That it was not quite 'by heart'?
Then He gives, in His wise and patient grace,
  That lesson again
With the mark still set in the self-same place.

Only, stay by His side
  Till the page is really known.
It may be we failed because we tried
  To learn it all alone,
And now that He would not let us lose
One lesson of love
(For He knows the loss),—can we refuse?

But oh! how could we dream
  That we knew it all so well!
Reading so fluently, as we deem,
  What we could not even spell!
And oh! how could we grieve once more
  That Patient One
Who has turned so many a task before!

That waiting One, who now
  Is letting us try again;
Watching us with the patient brow,
  That bore the wreath of pain;
Thoroughly teaching what He would teach,
  Line upon line,
Thoroughly doing His work in each.

Then let our hearts 'be still,'
  Though our task is turned to-day;
Oh let Him teach us what He will,
  In His own gracious way.
Till, sitting only at Jesus' feet,
  As we learn each line
The hardest is found all clear and sweet!

Sunday Night

Rest him, O Father! Thou didst send him forth
With great and gracious messages of love;
But Thy ambassador is weary now,

Worn with the weight of his high embassy.
Now care for him as Thou hast cared for us
In sending him; and cause him to lie down
In Thy fresh pastures, by Thy streams of peace.
Let Thy left hand be now beneath his head,
And Thine upholding right encircle him,
And, underneath, the Everlasting arms
Be felt in full support. So let him rest,
Hushed like a little child, without one care;
And so give Thy belovèd sleep to-night.

Rest him, dear Master! He hath poured for us
The wine of joy, and we have been refreshed.
Now fill his chalice, give him sweet new draughts
Of life and love, with Thine own hand; be Thou
His ministrant to-night; draw very near
In all Thy tenderness and all Thy power.
Oh speak to him! Thou knowest how to speak
A word in season to Thy weary ones,
And he is weary now. Thou lovest him—
Let Thy disciple lean upon Thy breast,
And, leaning, gain new strength to 'rise and shine.'

Rest him, O loving Spirit! Let Thy calm
Fall on his soul to-night. O holy Dove,
Spread Thy bright wing above him, let him rest
Beneath its shadow; let him know afresh
The infinite truth and might of Thy dear name—
'Our Comforter!' As gentlest touch will stay
The strong vibrations of a jarring chord,
So lay Thy hand upon his heart, and still
Each overstraining throb, each pulsing pain.
Then, in the stillness, breathe upon the strings,
And let thy holy music overflow
With soothing power his listening, resting soul.

A Song in the Night
[Written in severe pain, Sunday afternoon, October 8th, 1876, at
the Pension Wengen, Alps.]

I take this pain, Lord Jesus,
  From Thine own hand,
The strength to bear it bravely

Thou wilt command.

I am too weak for effort,
  So let me rest,
In hush of sweet submission,
  On Thine own breast.

I take this pain, Lord Jesus,
  As proof indeed
That Thou art watching closely
  My truest need;

That Thou, my Good Physician,
  Art watching still;
That all Thine own good pleasure
  Thou wilt fulfil.

I take this pain, Lord Jesus;
  What Thou dost choose
The soul that really loves Thee
  Will not refuse.

It is not for the first time
  I trust to-day;
For Thee my heart has never
  A trustless 'Nay!'

I take this pain, Lord Jesus;
  But what beside?
'Tis no unmingled portion
  Thou dost provide.

In every hour of faintness
  My cup runs o'er
With faithfulness and mercy,
  And love's sweet store.

I take this pain, Lord Jesus,
  As Thine own gift;
And true though tremulous praises
  I now uplift.

I am too weak to sing them,
  But Thou dost hear
The whisper from the pillow,
  Thou art so near!

'Tis Thy dear hand, O Saviour,

That presseth sore,
The hand that bears the nail-prints
  For evermore.

And now beneath its shadow,
  Hidden by Thee,
The pressure only tells me
  Thou lovest me!

What will You do without Him?

I could not do without Him!
  Jesus is more to me
Than all the richest, fairest gifts
  Of earth could ever be.
But the more I find Him precious—
  And the more I find Him true—
The more I long for you to find
  What He can be to you.

You need not do without Him,
  For He is passing by,
He is waiting to be gracious,
  Only waiting for your cry:
He is waiting to receive you—
  To make you all His own!
Why will you do without Him,
  And wander on alone?

Why will you do without Him?
  Is He not kind indeed?
Did He not die to save you?
  Is He not all you need?
Do you not want a Saviour?
  Do you not want a Friend?
One who will love you faithfully,
  And love you to the end?

Why will you do without Him?
  The Word of God is true!
The world is passing to its doom—
  And you are passing too.
It may be no to-morrow
  Shall dawn on you or me;
Why will you run the awful risk

Of all eternity?

What will you do without Him,
 In the long and dreary day
Of trouble and perplexity,
 When you do not know the way,
And no one else can help you,
 And no one guides you right,
And hope comes not with morning,
 And rest comes not with night?

You could not do without Him,
 If once He made you see
The fetters that enchain you,
 Till He hath set you free.
If once you saw the fearful load
 Of sin upon your soul;
The hidden plague that ends in death,
 Unless He makes you whole!

What will you do without Him,
 When death is drawing near?
Without His love—the only love
 That casts out every fear;
When the shadow-valley opens,
 Unlighted and unknown,
And the terrors of its darkness
 Must all be passed alone!

What will you do without Him,
 When the great white throne is set,
And the Judge who never can mistake,
 And never can forget,—
The Judge whom you have never here
 As Friend and Saviour sought,
Shall summon you to give account
 Of deed and word and thought?

What will you do without Him,
 When He hath shut the door,
And you are left outside, because
 You would not come before?
When it is no use knocking,
 No use to stand and wait;
For the word of doom tolls through your heart

That terrible 'Too late!'

You cannot do without Him!
  There is no other name
By which you ever can be saved,
  No way, no hope, no claim!
Without Him—everlasting loss
  Of love, and life, and light!
Without Him—everlasting woe,
  And everlasting night.

But with Him—oh! with Jesus!
  Are any words so blest?
With Jesus, everlasting joy
  And everlasting rest!
With Jesus—all the empty heart
  Filled with His perfect love;
With Jesus—perfect peace below,
  And perfect bliss above.

Why should you do without Him?
  It is not yet too late;
He has not closed the day of grace,
  He has not shut the gate.
He calls you! hush! He calls you!
  He would not have you go
Another step without Him,
  Because He loves you so.

Why will you do without Him?
  He calls and calls again—
'Come unto Me! Come unto Me!'
  Oh, shall He call in vain?
He wants to have you with Him;
  Do you not want Him too?
You cannot do without Him,
  And He wants—even you.

Church Missionary Jubilee Hymn

'He shall see of the travail of His soul, and shall be satisfied.'

—Isa. liii. 11.

Rejoice with Jesus Christ to-day,
All ye who love His holy sway!

The travail of His soul is past,
He shall be satisfied at last.

Rejoice with Him, rejoice indeed!
For He shall see His chosen seed.
But ours the trust, the grand employ,
To work out this divinest joy.

Of all His own He loseth none,
They shall be gathered one by one;
He gathereth the smallest grain,
His travail shall not be in vain.

Arise and work! arise and pray
That He would haste the dawning day!
And let the silver trumpet sound,
Wherever Satan's slaves are found.

The vanquished foe shall soon be stilled,
The conquering Saviour's joy fulfilled,
Fulfilled in us, fulfilled in them,
His crown, His royal diadem.

Soon, soon our waiting eyes shall see
The Saviour's mighty Jubilee!
His harvest joy is filling fast,
He shall be satisfied at last.

A Happy New Year to You!

New mercies, new blessings, new light on thy way;
New courage, new hope, and new strength for each day;
New notes of thanksgiving, new chords of delight,
New praise in the morning, new songs in the night,
New wine in thy chalice, new altars to raise;
New fruits for thy Master, new garments of praise;
New gifts from His treasures, new smiles from His face;
New streams from the Fountain of infinite grace;
New stars for thy crown, and new tokens of love;
New gleams of the glory that waits thee above;
New light of His countenance, full and unpriced;
All this be the joy of thy new life in Christ!

Another Year

Another year is dawning!
  Dear Master, let it be
In working or in waiting,
  Another year with Thee.

Another year of leaning
  Upon Thy loving breast,
Of ever-deepening trustfulness,
Of quiet, happy rest.

Another year of mercies,
  Of faithfulness and grace;
Another year of gladness
  In the shining of Thy face.

Another year of progress,
  Another year of praise;
Another year of proving
  Thy presence 'all the days.'

Another year of service,
  Of witness for Thy love;
Another year of training
  For holier work above.

Another year is dawning!
  Dear Master, let it be
On earth, or else in heaven,
  Another year for Thee!

New Year's Wishes

What shall I wish thee?
  Treasures of earth?
Songs in the springtime,
  Pleasure and mirth?
Flowers on thy pathway,
  Skies ever clear?
Would this ensure thee
  A Happy New Year?

What shall I wish thee?
  What can be found
Bringing thee sunshine
  All the year round?

Where is the treasure,
  Lasting and dear,
That shall ensure thee
  A Happy New Year?

Faith that increaseth,
  Walking in light;
Hope that aboundeth,
  Happy and bright;
Love that is perfect,
  Casting out fear;
These shall ensure thee
  A Happy New Year.

Peace in the Saviour,
  Rest at His feet,
Smile of His countenance
  Radiant and sweet,
Joy in His presence!
  Christ ever near!
This will ensure thee
  A Happy New Year!

'Most Blessed For Ever.'
(Though the date of these lines is uncertain, they are chosen as a
closing chord to her songs on earth.)

The prayer of many a day is all fulfilled,
Only by full fruition stayed and stilled;
You asked for blessing as your Father willed,
  Now He hath answered: 'Most blessed for ever!'

Lost is the daily light of mutual smile,
You therefore sorrow now a little while;
But floating down life's dimmed and lonely aisle
  Comes the clear music: 'Most blessed for ever!'

From the great anthems of the Crystal Sea,
Through the far vistas of Eternity,
Grand echoes of the word peal on for thee,
  Sweetest and fullest: 'Most blessed for ever.'

CPSIA information can be obtained
at www.ICGtesting.com
Printed in the USA
LVHW020329190520
656030LV00019B/1592